I HAD A ROW WITH A GERMAN

A BATTLE OF BRITAIN CASUALTY

I HAD A ROW WITH A GERMAN

A BATTLE OF BRITAIN CASUALTY

GROUP CAPTAIN THOMAS PERCY GLEAVE CBE

Introduced by Dilip Sarkar MBE, FRHistS

Foreword by Air Vice-Marshal Leigh-Mallory

AIR WORLD

AIR WORLD

I HAD A ROW WITH A GERMAN
A Battle of Britain Casualty

First published in Great Britain in 1941 by Macmillan & Co. Ltd.

This edition published 2022 by
Air World Books,
An imprint of
Pen & Sword Books Ltd,
Yorkshire - Philadelphia

Main text Copyright © Group Captain Thomas Percy Gleave CBE,
Introduction Copyright © Dilip Sarkar MBE, FRHistS
Foreword Copyright © Air Vice-Marshal Leigh-Mallory

ISBN 978 1 39907 273 1

The right of Group Captain Thomas Percy Gleave CBE to be identified as Author of this work has been asserted by him in accordance with the Copyright, Designs and Patents Act 1988. A CIP catalogue record for this book is available from the British Library All rights reserved.

No part of this book may be reproduced or transmitted in any form or by any means, electronic or mechanical including photocopying, recording or by any information storage and retrieval system, without permission from the Publisher in writing.

Typeset by SJmagic DESIGN SERVICES, India.
Printed and bound in the UK by CPI Group (UK) Ltd.

Pen & Sword Books Ltd incorporates the imprints of Pen & Sword Archaeology, Air World Books, Atlas, Aviation, Battleground, Discovery, Family History, History, Maritime, Military, Naval, Politics, Social History, Transport, True Crime, Claymore Press, Frontline Books, Praetorian Press, Seaforth Publishing and White Owl

For a complete list of Pen & Sword titles please contact:

PEN & SWORD BOOKS LTD
47 Church Street, Barnsley, South Yorkshire, S70 2AS, UK.
E-mail: enquiries@pen-and-sword.co.uk
Website: www.pen-and-sword.co.uk

Or

PEN AND SWORD BOOKS,
1950 Lawrence Road, Havertown, PA 19083, USA
E-mail: Uspen-and-sword@casematepublishers.com
Website: www.penandswordbooks.com

Contents

Introduction by Dilip Sarkar MBE, FRHistS — vi

Part I
THE JOURNEY TO PUBLICATION — 1

Part II
I HAD A ROW WITH A GERMAN — 27

Foreword by Air Vice-Marshal Leigh-Mallory — 29
Preface — 30
Chapter 1 I Make a Vow — 31
Chapter 2 The Black Cross — 57
Chapter 3 The Red Cross — 79
Chapter 4 The White Cross — 98
Acknowledgements — 100

Part III
AFTER PUBLICATION — 101

APPENDICES
Appendix I   Tom Gleave's Combat Reports — 145
Appendix II   Selected Wartime Reviews — 151
Appendix III Notes on Tom Gleave's Service Record — 162
Appendix IV   Tom Gleave's Decorations and Awards — 166

Introduction

by Dilip Sarkar MBE, FRHistS

Thomas Percy Gleave was born in in Liverpool on 6 September 1908, the second son of Arthur and Amy Gleave – and was an exceptional individual by any standards.

Privately educated at Westminster High and Liverpool Collegiate schools, Tom developed an early fascination for aeroplanes and in 1927 became a founder member of Merseyside Flying Club. On 6 July 1929, Tom was awarded his 'A' Licence to fly civilian aircraft, his mother having funded the lessons necessary to convert his dreams of flight to reality. Although the young aviator wanted to become a full-time pilot, he was persuaded to remain in the family tanning business, so spent six years 'making leather with flying as a sideline'.

In the summer of 1929, the adventurous Tom joined the Beardmore Tanning Company in Ontario, where he flew with the Toronto Flying Club. Although his father considered full-time flying far too dangerous an occupation, Tom was determined and applied to join the Royal Canadian Air Force. Only then did his father relent, but on the condition that Tom came home and joined the Royal Air Force. So it was that in September 1930, Tom Gleave accepted a Short Service Commission in the RAF, and after service flying training joined No 1 (Fighter) Squadron at Tangmere.

Flying single-engine biplane fighters, including the Siskin and Fury, Pilot Officer Gleave excelled at aerobatics, joining No 1 Squadron's aerobatic team. Ever intrepid, on 11 October 1933, Tom attempted to

INTRODUCTION

Pilot Officer Tom Gleave pictured whilst serving with No 1 Squadron at Tangmere in the 1930s.

Flight Lieutenant Tom Gleave married Miss Beryl Pitts in Chichester on 16 March 1935, the happy couple seen here on their wedding day.

INTRODUCTION

A 253 Squadron Hawker Hurricane.

become the first man to fly from England to Ceylon. Taking off from Lympne in a civilian Simmonds Spartan, four days later a downdraught forced him to 'land in a tree', in a Turkish ravine. The crash, Tom recalled, 'modified' his nose.

Back home, in 1934, with a rare 'exceptional' pilot rating, Tom became a flying instructor. In anticipation of war with Hitler's Germany, his commission changed to one of medium-term.

By December 1938, Tom was a squadron leader at Fighter Command HQ Operations Room, serving as one of three Bomber Liaison Officers. Having always been anxious to see action once war broke out, eventually, on 2 June 1940, the day the Dunkirk evacuation successfully concluded, Squadron Leader Gleave, by now a married man and a father, joined 253 Squadron as a 'supernumerary' officer to gain experience on the Hawker Hurricane monoplane fighter and current operational conditions.

What happened next was traumatic – and is the subject of this book. In sum, 253 Squadron was posted to Kenley during the Battle of Britain, suffering a number of casualties in the first few days, including the Commanding Officer, Squadron Leader Harold

Starr, who was shot down and killed on the morning of 31 August 1940. Having already temporarily commanded 253 previously, Tom assumed command, but was himself shot down in flames that afternoon.

Escaping from the furnace that his Hurricane cockpit rapidly became, and descending by parachute, the horrendously burned airman was taken in by the farming folk on whose land he had alighted. His main concern was the mess his wounds were making of Mrs Lewis's clean bed linen!

Although the journey in an open-top car to Orpington Hospital seemed an eternity to Tom, fifteen minutes after departing the Lewis farm he was admitted to into the care of its staff. On 3 September 1940, Tom's wife, Beryl, received a telegram in error informing her that her gallant husband had been admitted, but that his condition was 'not serious'. Nonetheless, Beryl rushed to Tom's bedside – finding him encased in dried Tannafax – and dangerously ill. Shocked and

The attendees of the first meeting of the Guinea Pig Club pictured outside the Surgeon's Mess on 20 July 1941. Left to right, they are Tom Gleave, Geoffrey Page, Russell Davies, Peter Weeks, John Hughes, Michael Coote, and Archibald McIndoe.

INTRODUCTION

Group Captain Tom Gleave in Paris with the surgeon Sir Archibald McIndoe – to whom he and other 'Guinea Pigs' owed so much. The extent of Tom's facial injuries are still all-too evident.

struggling to find words, Beryl laconically enquired 'What on earth have you been doing to yourself, darling?'

Tom's reply was priceless: 'Had a row with a German'.

So serious were Tom's injuries that he required specialist treatment at the now world famous 'Ward 3', the Burns Unit of the Queen Victoria Hospital at East Grinstead. He was moved there at the end of October 1940.

Under the care of the gifted surgeon Archibald McIndoe, Ward 3's patients were restored to good health in both mind and body, as Tom later recalled: 'Archie generated a bond of fellowship in which rank was forgotten. He believed that nothing could stand in the way of making terribly mutilated human beings whole again, and so we had much more freedom than was traditional in medical circles.'

On the afternoon of 20 July 1941, after a typical Ward 3 Saturday night 'thrash', a number of patients, amongst them Squadron Leader Tom Gleave, decided to form a drinking club. So it was that the

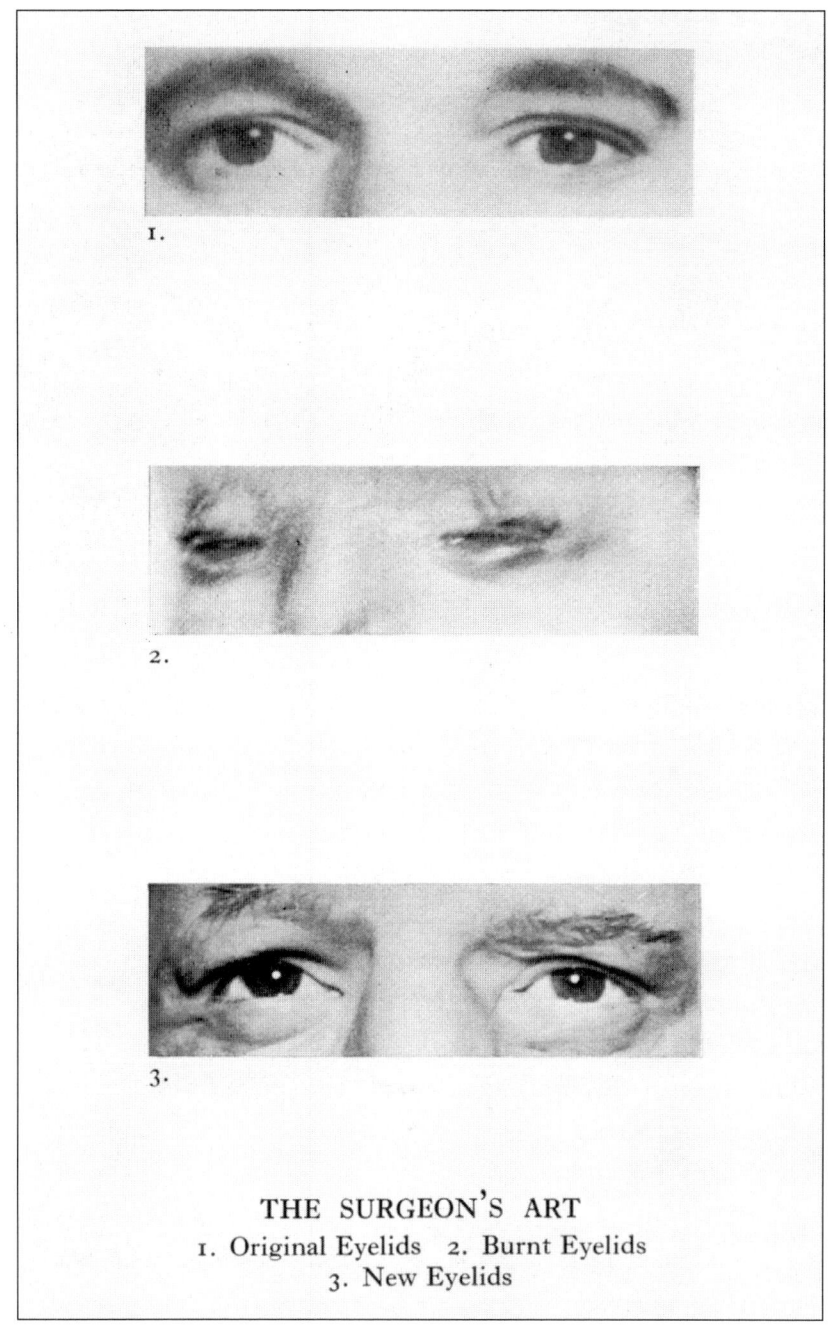

THE SURGEON'S ART
1. Original Eyelids 2. Burnt Eyelids
3. New Eyelids

The original caption to these three images states 'The Surgeon's Art: 1. Original eyelids; 2. Burnt eyelids; 3. New eyelids.'

INTRODUCTION

Group Captain Tom and Beryl Gleave pictured in later life.

'Guinea Pig Club' was formed, membership comprising wounded airmen treated by McIndoe. It would become far more than just a drinking club, however, and as Chief Guinea Pig, Tom, always supported by Beryl, would devote much time and energy over the years to ensuring the welfare of its members.

Tom's memoir *I Had A Row With A German* was published in 1941. It was amongst the first such accounts published and in advance of several published in 1942, including David Crook's well-known *Spitfire Pilot*, Brian Lane's ever-popular *Spitfire!*, 'Widge' Gleed's classic *Arise to Conquer*, and Richard Hillary's tour de force, *The Last Enemy*. Tom's account was well-received.

After many operations, which he would endure periodically for the rest of his life, Tom returned to active duty. In February 1942, Wing Commander Gleave was commanding RAF Manston during the infamous 'Channel Dash', when the Germans audaciously passed the cruisers *Scharnhorst*, *Gneisenau* and *Prinz Eugen* through the Dover Strait. It was Tom who waved off the six Fairey Swordfish

Some of Tom Gleave's papers, including *Eagles of Nemesis*, pictured during my visit.

biplane torpedo bombers led by Lieutenant Commander Eugene Esmonde. There were few survivors, Esmonde not amongst them – and it was Tom who successfully recommended this brave Fleet Air Arm pilot for a posthumous Victoria Cross.

Later that year, Tom was still commanding Manston during Operation *Jubilee*, the great combined operation during which a predominantly Canadian amphibious force was landed at Dieppe – suffering grave losses. That day, 19 August 1942, Manston, a coastal airfield in East Kent, became a hive of activity, as aircraft from far and wide put down to re-fuel. These were historic events – and Tom Gleave witnessed them first-hand.

Tom became a group captain on 5 September 1942 and was appointed 'Group Captain Air Plans' on the Special Planning Staff at Norfolk House, Portsmouth, working in Operation *Round-Up* – later to become *Overlord*, the Allied invasion of Normandy. Group

INTRODUCTION

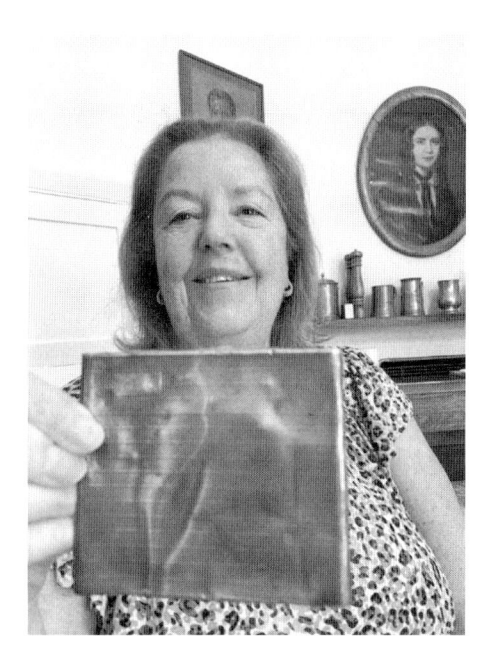

Right: Tom and Beryl Gleave's daughter, Angela Lodge, with the silver cigarette case her father was carrying when he was shot down and badly burned on 31 August 1940.

Below: A close-up of Tom's cigarette case.

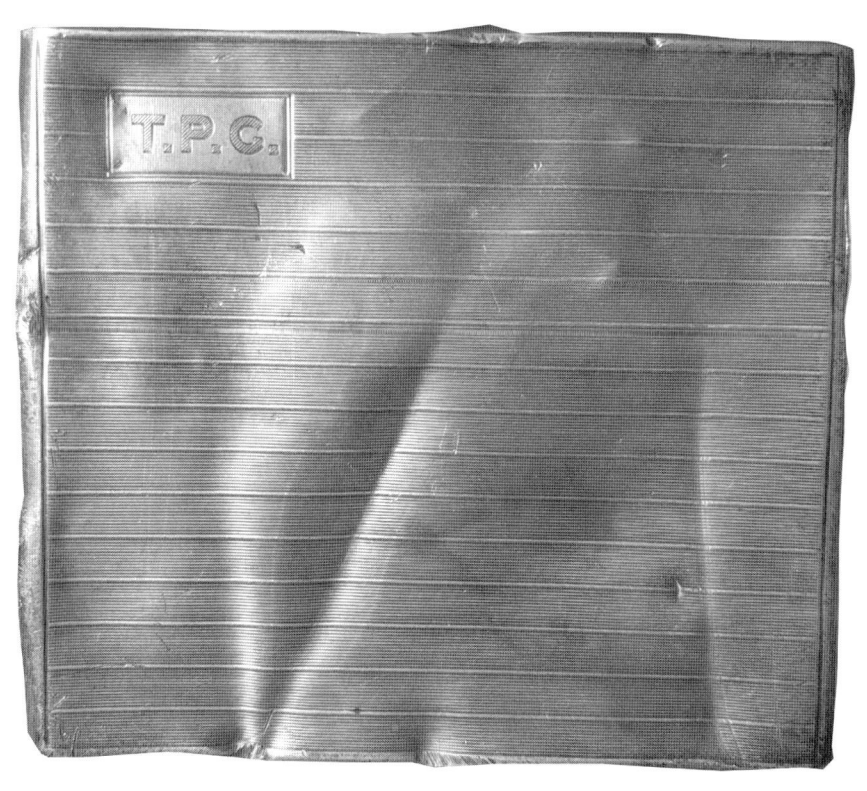

Tom Gleave's Battle of Britain pilot's flying logbook.

Captain Gleave remained on the staff at what became Supreme Headquarters Allied Expeditionary Force (SHAEF) until Germany surrendered, after which he became Senior Air Staff Officer to the RAF Delegation in France. Having subsequently served as Group Director at the RAF Staff College, Bracknell, Group Captain T.P. Gleave CBE was invalided out of the service in 1953 – as a direct consequence of his Battle of Britain injuries.

Thereafter, Tom became a Cabinet Office historian, working on the events of the Second World War in the Mediterranean and Middle East for thirty-five years. As a result of this endeavour, he was elected to the Fellowship of the Royal Historical Society (FRHistS) and in 1974 became a consultant to the Cabinet Office's official history he had spent so many years working on. He also became a committee member and later Deputy Chairman and Historian to the Battle of Britain Fighter Association, formed by and for Churchill's fabled 'Few' in 1968. Throughout, he continued his good work for the Guinea Pig Club.

INTRODUCTION

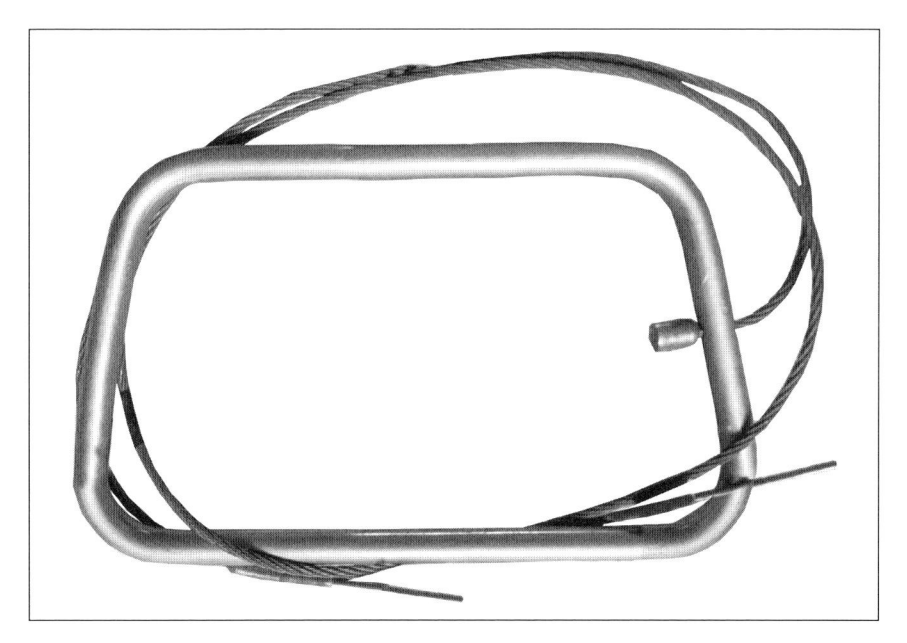

Tom Gleave's parachute D-ring which he discarded at Mace Farm, where, to the east of Biggin Hill, his Hurricane crashed on 31 August 1940. Subsequently recovered, it was duly presented back to him. (Courtesy of Robert Mitchell)

In 1967, the remains of the Hurricane Tom had baled out of on 31 August 1940, were recovered from Hazel Wood at Cudham by Biggin Hill's Flairavia Flying Club. It was an event that Tom attended in person, declaring the experience 'an interesting day'.

In 1968, Group Captain Gleave was amongst the technical consultants appointed to work on the film *Battle of Britain*. In 1990, he was featured in an episode of *This Is Your Life*, the popular Thames Television weekly biographical programme.

Tom Gleave passed away on 12 June 1993, aged eighty-four, having led by any standards a full and extraordinary life – during which he became a quiet but compelling inspiration and did nothing but good. As Tom himself said, 'I wouldn't have missed it for all the tea in China, to have taken part in the Battle of Britain and to have known Archibald McIndoe is more than many can achieve in one lifetime'.

I HAD A ROW WITH A GERMAN

DAILY EXPRESS MONDAY FEBRUARY 27 1967

PILOT FINDS PLANE 27 YEARS LATER

Express Staff Reporter

A PILOT was reunited yesterday with the Hurricane he parted company with 16,000ft. up during the Battle of Britain.

"That is my aircraft," said Group Captain Thomas Gleave as he stood among the ruins of the fighter plane which has lain rusted and forgotten on a Kent hillside for 27 years.

It exploded around him as he attacked a formation of German Ju 88 bombers over the famous wartime airfield at Biggin Hill.

The group captain, his face scarred by burns from the Hurricane's blazing cockpit, trudged in gumboots with his wife Beryl down the muddy hillside through the clutching tangle of hawthorn.

SPATTERED

He named the bits of wreckage —a piece of the undercarriage, part of a main spar, spattered with melted metal from the engine, a scrap of the starboard wing.

At the end of the trail of wreckage lay the Rolls-Royce Merlin engine.

But the 58-year-old group captain said: "This must be my plane though there is, naturally, nothing recognisable in the wreckage. It was seen to crash in exactly this place."

He told of that day—August 31, 1940: "It was a funny sort of day—blazingly hot but with a mist haze.

"The German formation was at 16,000 feet and we attacked the bomber from underneath. I was making my third attack when I got an incendiary in the starboard tank. Never knew where it came from.

"That day I knocked out a bomber's port engine — and that is all I can claim before baling out."

A newspaper cutting detailing the excavation of the crash site of Tom Gleave's Hurricane on 26 February 1967.

xviii

INTRODUCTION

A lump of once molten alloy from the wreckage of Tom's Hurricane, P3115, which, suitably mounted on a plinth, was presented to him. Note the small Hurricane that, visible centre right, was fashioned from the metal.

But then, perhaps, Tom reached out from beyond the grave.

In 2021, I was working on a new project *Forgotten Heroes of the Battle of Britain* (published by Pen & Sword in 2022), a substantial book, as always based upon detailed and comprehensive original research with primary sources, each chapter of which concerns a particular airman. Tom Gleave, I thought, was a well-known name, not least because of his book, although published under the pseudonym 'RAF Casualty'. But how much did we really know about him?

Being a Fellow of the Royal Historical Society myself, I was also interested in Tom for that reason, because he too was a historian. So it was that one summer's day I found myself sat with Tom's daughter, Angela, and son-in-law, Tim, at what was once Tom and Beryl's Thameside Maidenhead home.

Over the last forty years I must have traced countless families, survivors and the relatives of casualties, and discovered a plethora of previously unpublished material, including memoirs, letters, diaries and photographs. Indeed, it never ceases to amaze me what treasures remain out there, hidden away, often forgotten about, in drawers and attics. Discovering and sharing such unique material has long been a personal passion, and you might assume that there would be nothing left undiscovered regarding someone so well-known as Tom Gleave – who himself wrote hundreds of historical articles and contributed to

A piece of Tom's Hurricane's engine, presented to him by the Essex Aviation Group. The substantial Rolls-Royce Merlin from P3115 can be seen today at IWM Duxford.

INTRODUCTION

The Merlin engine from Tom's Hurricane P3115, which was coded SW-K, as can be seen at IWM Duxford. P3115 crashed at Mace Farm, east of Biggin Hill, from where this engine was recovered by a local flying group in the 1960s. (Courtesy of Robert Mitchell)

many publications. Wrong: here was a veritable treasure trove of historical material indeed, laid out for my inspection on the dining table in what was now Angela and Tim's home.

Amongst the piles of papers were both the original, unedited, manuscript of this book, and a much more substantial, wider, unpublished memoir. And I learned something: Tom's original title for this book was *Eagles of Nemesis* – changed by the publisher,

Above left: Tom Gleave's Guinea Pig Club wall plaque.

Above right: Tom Gleave's Battle of Britain Fighter Association wall plaque.

Macmillan, to *I Had A Row With A German*. There were other treasures too, photographs, including a superb one of Tom with Archibald McIndoe in Paris, and even artefacts from Tom's Hurricane. Extraordinary! Suffice it to say that this material provided for Tom's chapter in *Forgotten Heroes* to be extremely detailed and much of it in his own words. Wonderful.

This also got me thinking. For a while, my great friend and Commissioning Editor Martin Mace and I had been discussing me producing a multi-volume history of the Battle of Britain, based upon my own extensive archival material, which would be my legacy after a lifetime researching the Battle. This body of work, I felt, could also support the Battle of Britain Memorial Trust, which achieved, and is responsible for, the National Memorial to The Few at Capel-le-Ferne, near Folkestone. Indeed, I have long been a supporter of the Trust and as a 'Friend of The Few', am always keen to promote and support the cause.

In due course it was agreed that the series would become the Trust's official history of the Battle of Britain – an honour, and a

INTRODUCTION

project I am currently working on. For charities like the Trust, raising awareness and public engagement is crucial, and that planted another seed, inspired in part by Angela and Tim sharing Tom's material. The Battle of Britain is a huge story, and history is made by people – so why not float a project as a partnership between the Trust and Pen & Sword aimed at encouraging the public to contribute and share relevant family archival material with a view to inclusion in the new official history? This idea was enthusiastically supported by all and 'Battle of Britain: The People's Project' went live on 10 July 2022, the 82nd anniversary of the Battle of Britain's start-date.

And so, Tom Gleave has once more played his part in inspiring and initiating a most important historical project …

Dilip Sarkar MBE, FRHistS, 2022

For more information regarding the Project, please see:
www.battleofbritainpeoplesproject.com

PART I

THE JOURNEY TO PUBLICATION

The following images form part of the substantial material in Tom Gleave's archive which remains in the care of Tom's daughter, Angela, and son-in-law, Tim. The documents they show present a fascinating insight into the process that Tom went through to have his book published in 1941.

D.S.

THE JOURNEY TO PUBLICATION

Tom's original typed manuscript for this book. He initially gave it the title *Eagles of Nemesis* and subtitle *The War-life of a pilot of the Royal Air Force who was shot down in flames during the Battle of Britain*. As can be seen, it was Tom who gave himself the pseudonym 'R.A.F. Casualty'.

I HAD A ROW WITH A GERMAN

> COPY.
>
>   'Sunnyside',
>   Westgate,
>   Chichester.
>
>   27th June, 1941.
>
> My Dear Lord Riverdale,
>
>   Last August I became an R.A.F. casualty, having been shot down in flames during the Battle of Britain. Since then I have been a patient, at first in a War Hospital and latterly in a special Burns and Skin Grafting Unit. By the end of August I hope to be back on duty, fit and strong again, my burns healed and with a 'new face'. You can no doubt appreciate my gratitude to those who have done so much for me, but unfortunately I am not financially affluent, nor have I the status whereby I could do something in a big way to repay a little of the debt I owe.
>
>   During the time I have spent out of Hospital, between operations, I have written a book with the intention of presenting it to the

The first of three pages of a copy of a letter that Tom sent to Lord Riverdale at the RAF Benevolent Fund on 27 June 1941. In this correspondence, he is offering the manuscript as a means of supporting the organisation's work in one manner or another. Lord Riverdale was, at the time, the Chairman of the RAF Benevolent Fund's Appeals Committee.

THE JOURNEY TO PUBLICATION

> Royal Air Force Benevolent Fund for publication in aid thereof. This book is the true story of my war-life, touching practically every sphere of R.A.F. activity, including, of course, the Battle of Britain. I have illustrated my writings with various photographs taken from Aeronautical Journals and other sources, and do not anticipate any difficulty in obtaining permission to publish them as there is no personal gain in doing so.
>
> I make no claims as a scholar, nor as a writer, but as it is a story concerning events which the public know only from the spectator's viewpoint I ventured to consider that, from the standpoint of one who was privileged to be 'on the field', it would appeal to them.
>
> At the moment I am engaged in the final editing of the manuscript and the typing of the fair copy prior to submitting it to the R.A.F. censors. It is my intention to ask my A.O.C. to write a foreword to the book when completed, which

The second page of the letter to Lord Riverdale. As well as outlining some of his book's content, it can be seen that Tom also passes judgement on his abilities as an author.

> will be, I hope, before I return to Hospital on July 7th. next.
>
> Should this proposition interest you, I should be grateful if you would inform me accordingly, and would be more than glad to present the book in its entirety to the R.A.F. Benevolent Fund for publication, or to arrange publication as you may advise.
>
> I make only one request - that the book remain anonymous.
>
> Yours sincerely,
>
> (Sgd.) T.P. GLEAVE.

The last page of the letter Tom sent to the RAF Benevolent Fund. Note how he ends by reinforcing his wish to remain anonymous.

THE JOURNEY TO PUBLICATION

> **THE ROYAL AIR FORCE BENEVOLENT FUND**
>
> PATRON: H.M. THE KING.
> PRESIDENT: H.R.H. THE DUKE OF GLOUCESTER, K.G.
> CHAIRMAN OF COUNCIL: H.R.H. THE DUKE OF KENT, K.G.
>
> CHAIRMAN OF APPEALS COMMITTEE
> THE RT. HON. LORD RIVERDALE.
>
> HONORARY SECRETARY
> BERTRAM T. RUMBLE.
>
> TELEPHONE: SLOANE 1681.
>
> 1 SLOANE STREET,
> LONDON. S.W.1.
>
> 1st July 1941.
>
> Wing Commander T.P. Gleave, R.A.F.,
> "Sunnyside",
> Westgate,
> Chichester,
> Sussex.
>
> Dear Wing Commander Gleave,
>
> Lord Riverdale has asked me to write and thank you for your letter to him of June 27th.
>
> He thinks it is perfectly marvellous for you to wish to do what you suggest in aid of the Royal Air Force Benevolent Fund.
>
> He also asks me to say how greatly pleased he is that you are now nearly restored to health.
>
> Neither he nor I know the processes through which you have to pass to obtain permission from the Air Council to your proposals, but no doubt you know the right avenue to explore.
>
> It may be that you should first of all submit your proposals to Air Commodore Harold Peake, the Director of Public Relations.
>
> Will you do that, or shall I?
>
> Yours sincerely,
>
> Bertram T. Rumble
>
> Hon. Secretary.

The RAF Benevolent Fund, in the shape of its Honorary Secretary, Bertram T. Rumble, replied quickly, as this letter dated 1 July 1941 testifies. Needless to say, the response to Tom's offer was extremely positive.

I HAD A ROW WITH A GERMAN

> 3rd July, 1941.
>
> Dear Mr Rumble
>
> Thank you very much for your letter of the 1st instant. Would you please thank Lord Riverdale on my behalf for his kind message.
>
> I was naturally very pleased to know of your attitude towards my proposition, and only hope the bo[ok] will be good enough!
>
> Would you kindly contact Air Commodore Peak as you suggest in your letter, and let me know the result. I return to Hospital on Monday, when I hope [to] obtain certain photographs which will complete the bo[ok]
>
> Maybe, if I am not required there immediate[ly] I could travel as far as London to see you personally
>
> My hospital address is - The Queen Victoria Cottage Hospital, East Grinstead, Sussex.
>
> Yours sincerely,
> T. P. Gleave

Tom replied to Bertram T. Rumble two days later – this being a copy of that letter dated 3 July 1941.

8

THE JOURNEY TO PUBLICATION

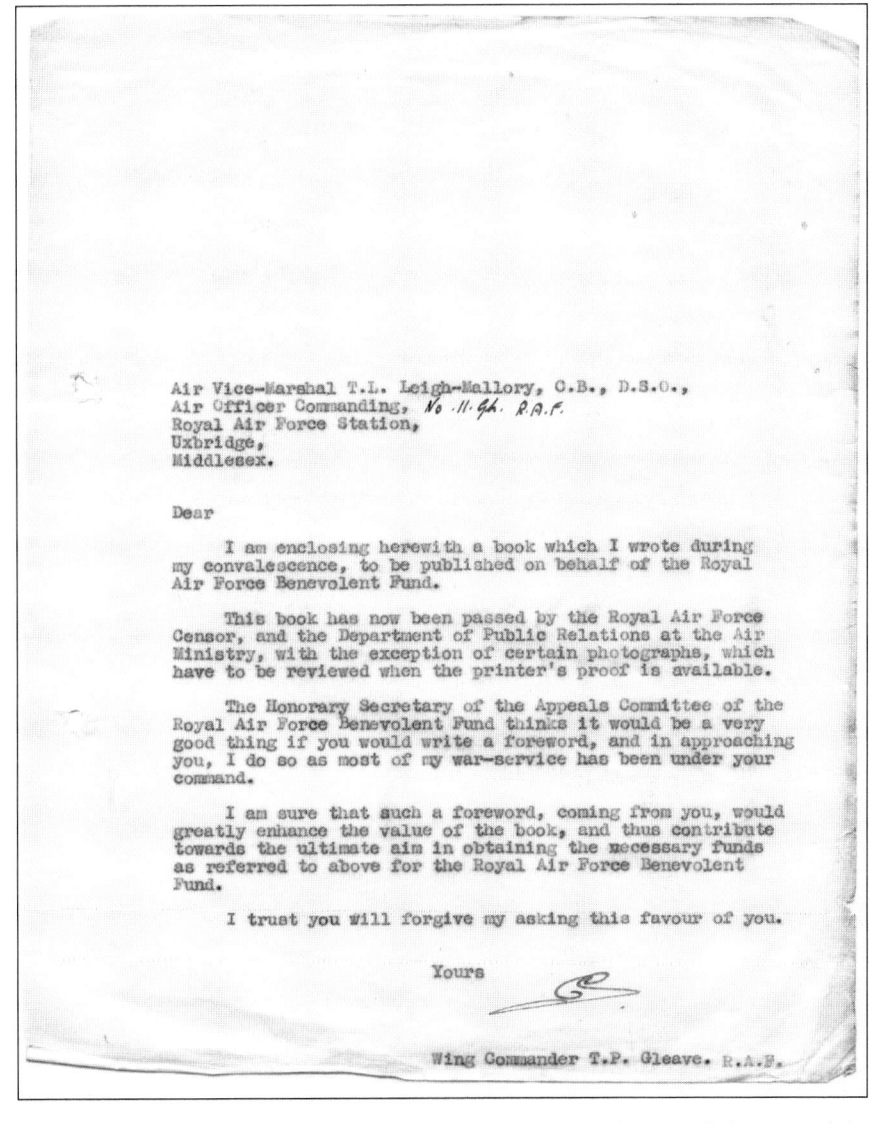

> Air Vice-Marshal T.L. Leigh-Mallory, C.B., D.S.O.,
> Air Officer Commanding, No. 11 Gp. R.A.F.
> Royal Air Force Station,
> Uxbridge,
> Middlesex.
>
> Dear
>
> I am enclosing herewith a book which I wrote during my convalescence, to be published on behalf of the Royal Air Force Benevolent Fund.
>
> This book has now been passed by the Royal Air Force Censor, and the Department of Public Relations at the Air Ministry, with the exception of certain photographs, which have to be reviewed when the printer's proof is available.
>
> The Honorary Secretary of the Appeals Committee of the Royal Air Force Benevolent Fund thinks it would be a very good thing if you would write a foreword, and in approaching you, I do so as most of my war-service has been under your command.
>
> I am sure that such a foreword, coming from you, would greatly enhance the value of the book, and thus contribute towards the ultimate aim in obtaining the necessary funds as referred to above for the Royal Air Force Benevolent Fund.
>
> I trust you will forgive my asking this favour of you.
>
> Yours
>
> Wing Commander T.P. Gleave. R.A.F.

At some point in the proceedings, Tom wrote to Air Vice-Marshal T.L. Leigh-Mallory, AOC 11 Group, at RAF Uxbridge, enquiring whether he would consider providing a foreword for the book. This copy of that letter is undated.

> Tel. No. ABBEY 3411.
> EXT. 5186
>
> AIR MINISTRY,
> KING CHARLES STREET,
> WHITEHALL, S.W.1.
>
> P.R.4/A.102
>
> 15th July, 1941.
>
> Dear Gleave,
>
> Thank you for your letter of the 14th July, forwarding the script of your proposed book "Eagles of Nemesis". We are now having it examined from a service suitability and security point of view and hope to let you have it back before long. I suggest that you should use a nom-de-plume as an indication of authorship, as it is a present rule that service personnel may not write on service matters under their own name and rank.
>
> As a matter of form we should like to see the photographs you propose to publish — I think that permission for any reproductions from "The Battle of Britain" should be obtained from the Ministry of Information.
>
> Please let me know if I an be of any further help to you.
>
> Yours sincerely,
>
> Bentley Beaman
>
> Wing Commander T.P. Gleave,
> Queen Victoria Cottage Hospital,
> East Grinstead, Sussex.

A letter sent from the Air Ministry to Tom on 15 July 1941, at which point he was at East Grinstead once again, explaining that they were examining his manuscript. The writer also points out how Tom could deal with the copyright of some of the images he wished to use.

THE JOURNEY TO PUBLICATION

```
TELEGRAMS "PUBLISH LESQUARE LONDON"          MACMILLAN & CO. LTD.
    CABLES "PUBLISH LONDON"
  TELEPHONE. WHITEHALL 8831                    ST MARTIN'S STREET,
  CODE- 5TH AND 6TH EDITIONS. A.B.C.
    PLEASE QUOTE                                LONDON, W.C.2.
         LD/JS                                 28th July, 1941.


         Wing-Commander T. F. Gleave,
         Ambergate,
         Dowhills Road,
         Blundellsands,
         Liverpool, 23.

         Dear Wing-Commander Gleave,

                 Thank you for your letter of July 25th
         enclosing Miss Hollender's note. Your proposal
         sounds interesting, and I should like an opportunity
         to discuss it with you on your way through London.
         I shall be here all this week, and if you telephone
         on arrival we can fix a time convenient to us both.

                 I need not remind you that there have,
         of course, been a number of books on the R.A.F.
         already, some of them quite successful. This does
         not preclude others, but it does set a fairly high
         standard. Your experiences, however, have been
         full, and I shall be glad in any event to answer
         any questions about publication which might be of
         help to you.

                     Yours sincerely,

                     Lovat Dickson.
```

On 28 July 1941, Tom received a letter from one Lovat Dickson at Macmillan & Co. in London, expressing initial interest in publishing his memoir. Horatio Henry Lovat Dickson was undoubtedly a man of the Empire. He was born in Victoria, Australia, on 30 June 1902, but moved with his family to Rhodesia (now Zimbabwe) when he was seven. When he turned eleven, he attended school in the UK, before, at fifteen, he headed to Canada. He founded and edited the Blue Diamond Mine newsletter while in Jasper, the start of a remarkable writing and publishing career. Lovat joined the staff of Macmillan & Co. in 1938. By 1940, he had become a director and the following year he was appointed the company's general manager, a position he held until his retirement in 1964. He is described as being 'the first Canadian to have a major publishing role in Britain'.

I HAD A ROW WITH A GERMAN

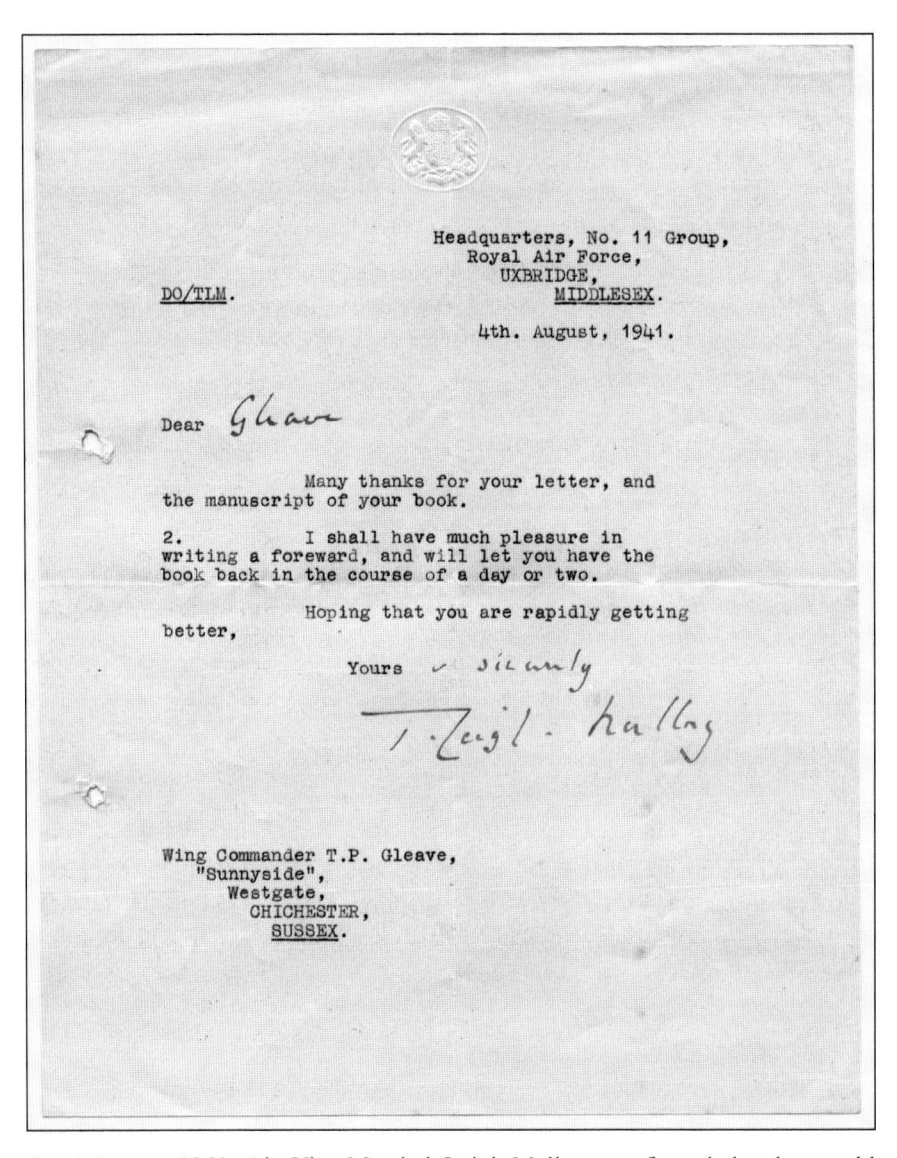

> Headquarters, No. 11 Group,
> Royal Air Force,
> UXBRIDGE,
> MIDDLESEX.
>
> DO/TLM.
>
> 4th. August, 1941.
>
> Dear Gleave,
>
> Many thanks for your letter, and the manuscript of your book.
>
> 2. I shall have much pleasure in writing a foreward, and will let you have the book back in the course of a day or two.
>
> Hoping that you are rapidly getting better,
>
> Yours very sincerely
>
> T. Leigh-Mallory
>
> Wing Commander T.P. Gleave,
>   "Sunnyside",
>   Westgate,
>   CHICHESTER,
>   SUSSEX.

On 4 August 1941, Air Vice-Marshal Leigh-Mallory confirmed that he would indeed provide a foreword to Tom's book.

THE JOURNEY TO PUBLICATION

Among the many suggestions that Tom made regarding the format of his book was the inclusion of a drawing or cartoon that was drawn by Tom Webster. The son of an ironmonger, Gilbert Tom Webster was a self-taught artist. In 1912 Webster moved to London to work as a political cartoonist on the *Daily Citizen*, whilst also working for the *Daily News and Star* and *Golf Illustrated*. Other papers he worked for included the *London Evening News* and *Daily Mail*. This telegram, also dated 4 August 1941, was sent by Tom, to Tom, confirming that the artwork was ready.

I HAD A ROW WITH A GERMAN

The cartoon that Tom Webster completed for, and dedicated to, Tom Gleave.

THE JOURNEY TO PUBLICATION

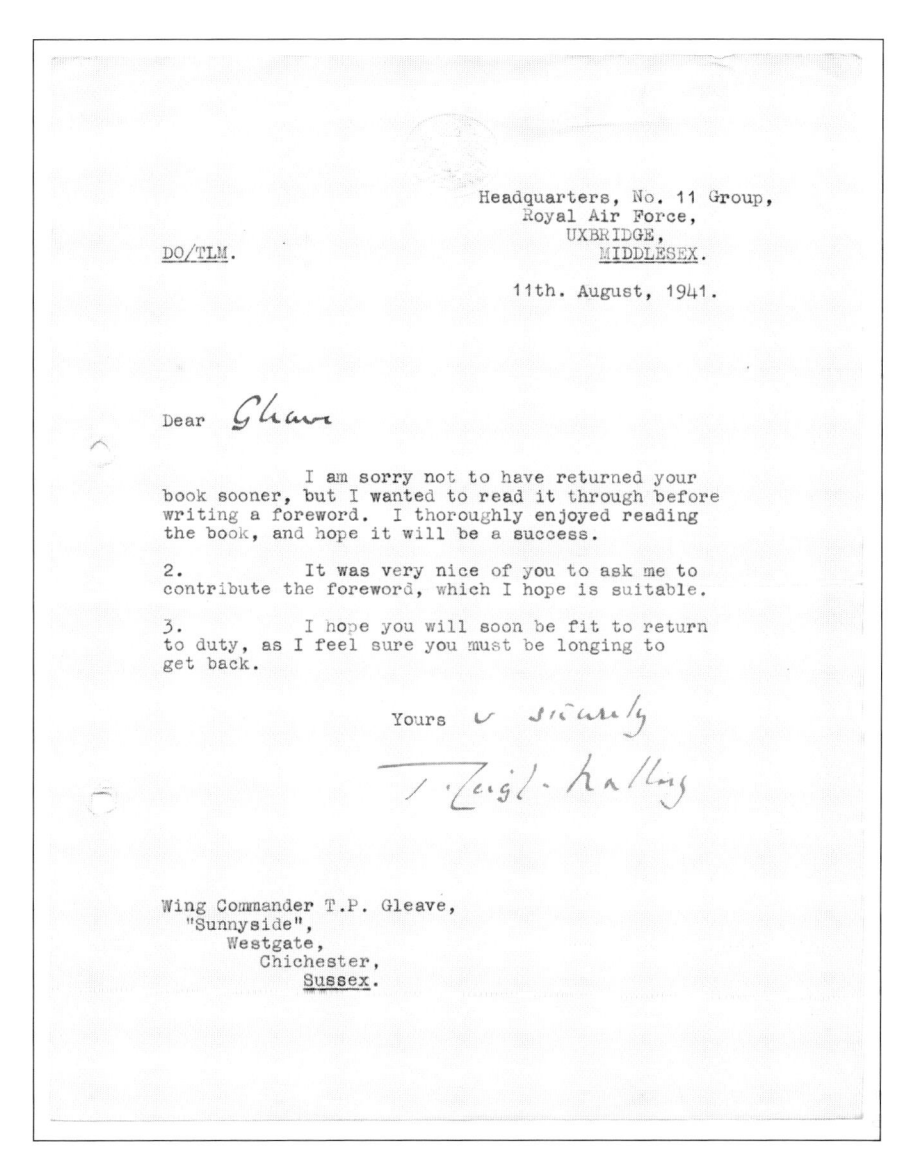

> DO/TLM.
>
> Headquarters, No. 11 Group,
> Royal Air Force,
> UXBRIDGE,
> MIDDLESEX.
>
> 11th. August, 1941.
>
> Dear Gleave
>
> I am sorry not to have returned your book sooner, but I wanted to read it through before writing a foreword. I thoroughly enjoyed reading the book, and hope it will be a success.
>
> 2. It was very nice of you to ask me to contribute the foreword, which I hope is suitable.
>
> 3. I hope you will soon be fit to return to duty, as I feel sure you must be longing to get back.
>
> Yours sincerely
>
> T. Leigh-Mallory
>
> Wing Commander T.P. Gleave,
> "Sunnyside",
>   Westgate,
>   Chichester,
>   Sussex.

Air Vice-Marshal Leigh-Mallory wrote to Tom again on 11 August 1941. In this letter he noted how much he had enjoyed the manuscript.

I HAD A ROW WITH A GERMAN

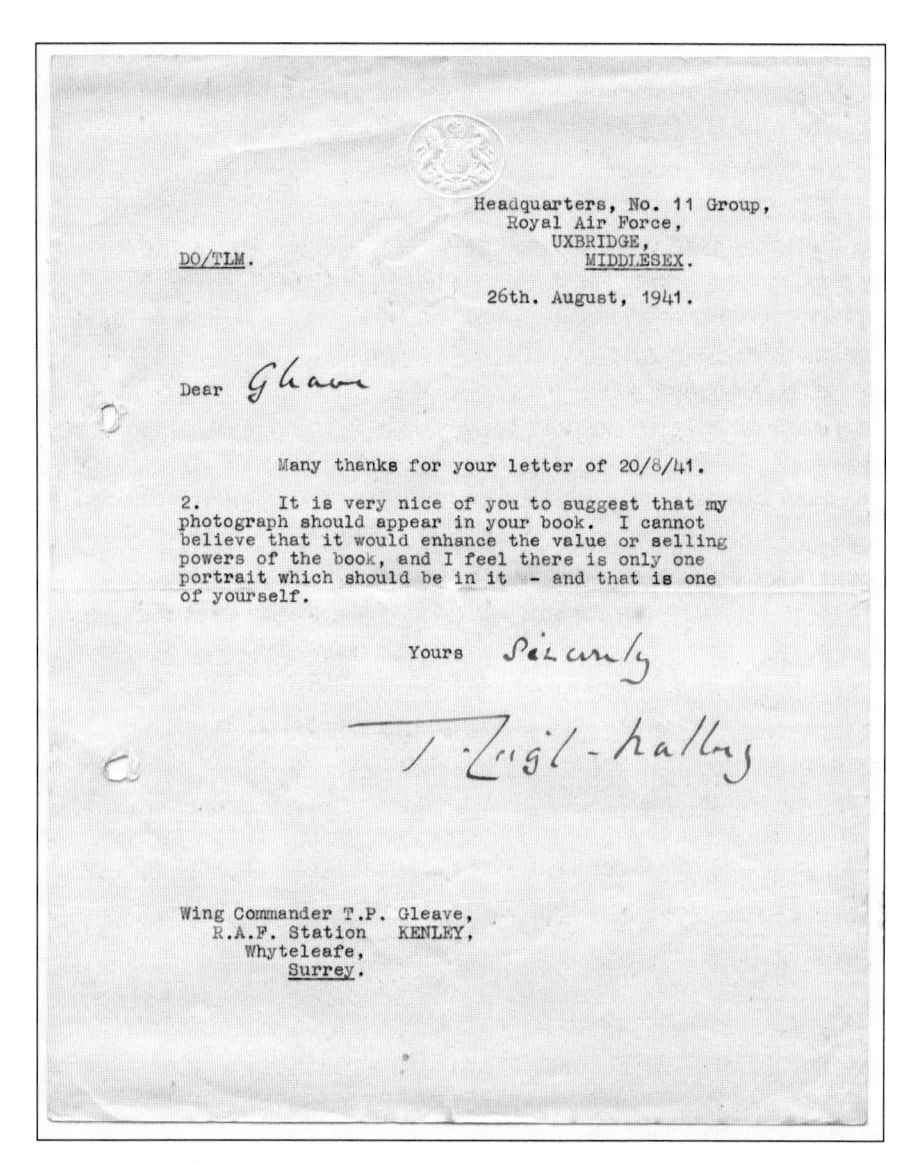

> DO/TLM.
>
> Headquarters, No. 11 Group,
> Royal Air Force,
> UXBRIDGE,
> MIDDLESEX.
>
> 26th. August, 1941.
>
> Dear Gleave
>
> Many thanks for your letter of 20/8/41.
>
> 2. It is very nice of you to suggest that my photograph should appear in your book. I cannot believe that it would enhance the value or selling powers of the book, and I feel there is only one portrait which should be in it - and that is one of yourself.
>
> Yours sincerely
>
> T. Leigh-Mallory
>
> Wing Commander T.P. Gleave,
> R.A.F. Station KENLEY,
> Whyteleafe,
> Surrey.

Another letter from Air Vice-Marshal Leigh-Mallory, this time politely pointing out why the AOC 11 Group's portrait should not appear in the book.

THE JOURNEY TO PUBLICATION

>
> MACMILLAN & CO. LTD.
> ST. MARTIN'S STREET,
> LONDON, W.C.2.
>
> TELEGRAMS: "PUBLISH, LESQUARE, LONDON"
> CABLES: "PUBLISH, LONDON"
> TELEPHONE: WHITEHALL 8831
> CODE: 5TH AND 6TH EDITIONS A.B.C
>
> PLEASE QUOTE LD/JS
>
> 27th August, 1941
>
> Wing-Commander T. P. Gleave,
> R.A.F. Officer's Mess,
> Kenley,
> Surrey.
>
> Dear Wing-Commander Gleave,
>
> We have now had an opportunity to examine carefully EAGLES OF NEMESIS, and we have decided that we should like to publish the book. There are a number of things in connection with it about which I should like to talk to you, and I wonder whether there is a chance of your being in London within the next day or two. If not, perhaps you could telephone me, and we could have a talk then.
>
> Yours sincerely,
>
> Lovat Dickson.

The letter from Lovat Dickson which, dated 27 August 1941, confirmed that Macmillan & Co. were interested in publishing *Eagles of Nemesis*.

I HAD A ROW WITH A GERMAN

> TELEGRAMS: "PUBLISH, LESQUARE, LONDON"
> CABLES: "PUBLISH, LONDON"
> TELEPHONE: WHITEHALL 8831
> CODE: 5TH AND 6TH EDITIONS A.B.C
>
> MACMILLAN & CO. LTD.
> ST. MARTIN'S STREET,
> LONDON, W.C.2.
>
> PLEASE QUOTE LD/VP
>
> 3rd September, 1941.
>
> Wing-Commander T.P. Gleave,
> R.A.F. Officers' Mess,
> Kenley,
> Surrey.
>
> Dear Wing-Commander Gleave,
>
> I enclose herewith the contract for EAGLES OF NEMESIS which I think is perfectly clear. The terms are in accordance with those we discussed. Would you sign this and let us have it back and we will then send you the counterpart for your retention.
>
> Yours sincerely,
>
> Lovat Dickson.
>
> Enclosure.

Tom Gleave received the draft contract for what was still called *Eagles of Nemesis* on 3 September 1941.

THE JOURNEY TO PUBLICATION

```
TELEGRAMS: "PUBLISH, LESQUARE, LONDON"         MACMILLAN & CO. LTD.
    CABLES: "PUBLISH, LONDON"                    ST. MARTIN'S STREET,
  TELEPHONE: WHITEHALL 8831
    CODE: 5TH AND 6TH EDITIONS A.B.C             LONDON, W.C.2.

      PLEASE QUOTE LD/JS              5th September, 1941.


            Wing-Commander T. P. Gleave,
            R. A. F. Officers' Mess,
            Kenley, Surrey.


            Dear Wing-Commander Gleave,

                        Thank you for your letter
            enclosing the cartoon and the two
            negatives.

                        Thank you, too, for the
            list of suggested titles for the book.
            I am putting these on one side for the
            moment, and we shall consider them
            together with any other suggestions
            made by our advisers. I hope to
            let you know about this next week.

                        Yours sincerely,

                        Lovat Dickson

                        Lovat Dickson.
```

One of the early discussions between Tom Gleave and Lovat Dickson must have involved a debate surrounding the manuscript's original title, as this letter, dated 5 September 1941, mentions the existence of a list of alternatives.

I HAD A ROW WITH A GERMAN

> TELEGRAMS: "PUBLISH, LESQUARE, LONDON"
> CABLES: "PUBLISH, LONDON"
> TELEPHONE: WHITEHALL 8831
> CODE: 5TH AND 6TH EDITIONS A.B.C
>
> MACMILLAN & CO. LTD.
> ST. MARTIN'S STREET,
> LONDON, W.C.2.
>
> PLEASE QUOTE LD/VP
>
> 9th September, 1941.
>
> Wing Commander T.P. Gleave,
> Officers' Mess,
> R.A.F. Station,
> Whiteleafe,
> Surrey.
>
> Dear Wing-Commander Gleave,
>
> I enclose herewith the contract for EAGLES OF NEMESIS signed by the Chairman of the Company. This copy is for your retention.
>
> What do you think of the title I HAD A ROW WITH A GERMAN for your book? This is the remark you made to your wife when she came to see you in hospital, and it has been suggested by an adviser as most suitable for the book.
>
> Yours sincerely,
>
> Lovat Dickson

On 9 September 1941, Lovat Dickson wrote to Tom Gleave enclosing a draft contract. Lovat also took the opportunity to suggest a new title: *I Had a Row With a German*.

> TELEGRAMS: "PUBLISH, LESQUARE, LONDON"
> CABLES: "PUBLISH, LONDON"
> TELEPHONE: WHITEHALL 8831
> CODE: 5TH AND 6TH EDITIONS A B C
>
> MACMILLAN & CO. LTD.
> ST. MARTIN'S STREET,
> LONDON, W.C.2.
>
> PLEASE QUOTE LD/VP   26th September, 1941
>
> Wing-Commander T.P. Gleave,
> R.A.F. Officers' Mess,
> Kenley, Surrey.
>
> Dear Wing-Commander Gleave,
>
> We feel here that Tom Webster's cartoon is not good enough to include in the book. The text of the book is admirable, and the photographs we have chosen to go with it suit the text. But this cartoon is not of the same standard, and although Tom Webster's name is a good one, we don't feel that it will help the book to include this as an illustration. I hope it does not place you in a too embarrassing position to have to tell him that it will not be used.
>
> Yours sincerely,
>
> Lovat Dickson.
>
> Enclosure.

After due consideration, it was felt by Lovat Dickson and his team that Tom Webster's cartoon should not be included within the book – as this letter dated 26 September 1941 reveals.

I HAD A ROW WITH A GERMAN

> TELEGRAMS: "PUBLISH, LESQUARE, LONDON"
> CABLES: "PUBLISH, LONDON"
> TELEPHONE: WHITEHALL 8831
> CODE: 5TH AND 6TH EDITIONS A.B.C
>
> MACMILLAN & CO. LTD.
> ST. MARTIN'S STREET,
> LONDON, W.C.2.
>
> PLEASE QUOTE HC/NH
>
> 29th September, 1941
>
> Wing-Commander T.P. Gleave,
> Officer's Mess,
> Royal Air Force,
> Northolt,
> Middx.
>
> Dear Sir
>
> **I Had a Row With a German**
>
> Mr. Lovat-Dickson has asked us to reply to your letter dated 26th September. We shall be very pleased to reproduce your portrait by Captain Orde as the frontispiece to your book, but before going ahead there is one point upon which we think it necessary to be quite clear. You mention that the charcoal portrait is your own property, but ownership does not necessarily endow you with copyright unless the picture was commissioned by you, and if this was not the case we think it would be advisable for you to get in touch with Captain Orde asking whether he would be agreeable for the reproduction to be made.
>
> We should also like to take the opportunity of asking whether you have received permission to reproduce the photograph you entitle "The Salt-Bath Unit and Crew" as we notice it is marked "Copyright by Nursing Mirror"?
>
> We are, Yours faithfully,
> for MACMILLAN & CO., LTD.

As this letter of 29 September 1941 indicates production of Tom's book was getting underway. In this instance there is some discussion surrounding two possible illustrations. The Orde portrait (which can be seen at the beginning of Part II) did make the first edition; the 'salt bath' picture did not. On this occasion, the letter was posted to the Officers' Mess at RAF Northolt.

THE JOURNEY TO PUBLICATION

TELEGRAMS: "PUBLISH, LESQUARE, LONDON"
CABLES: "PUBLISH, LONDON"
TELEPHONE: WHITEHALL 8831
CODE: 5TH AND 6TH EDITIONS A.B.C

MACMILLAN & CO. LTD.
ST. MARTIN'S STREET,
LONDON, W.C.2.

PLEASE QUOTE **LD/VP**

14th October, 1941.

Wing-Commander T.P. Gleave,
Officers' Mess,
Doon House,
Royal Air Force,
Manston, Kent.

Dear Wing-Commander Gleave,

    Thank you for your letter. It is quite evident, from what you say, that the portrait is your property.

    The book is progressing as well as can be expected in these most difficult times. We expect to have advance copies by the middle of November, and anticipate publishing, if no accident intervenes, about the end of November.

                Yours sincerely,

                Lovat Dickson.

In this from Lovat Dickson dated 14 October 1941, Tom was provided with an initial guide as to when his book might be ready for publication. This letter was sent to Tom c/o the Officers' Mess (Doon House) at RAF Manston.

I HAD A ROW WITH A GERMAN

> MACMILLAN & CO., LTD.
> ST MARTIN'S STREET,
> LONDON, W.C.2
>
> 22nd October, 1941
>
> LD/JS
>
> Wing-Commander T. P. Gleave,
> Officers' Mess,
> Doon House,
> Royal Air Force,
> Manston, Kent.
>
> Dear Wing-Commander Gleave,
>
> Thank you for your letter. We have decided not to use the picture of yourself in the salt-bath, and it won't therefore be necessary to approach *The Nursing Mirror*. We have eight good photographs without that.
>
> We have included in the blurb on the jacket an italicised note that all the author's royalties on the book are to go to the R.A.F. Benevolent Fund.
>
> Yours sincerely,
>
> Lovat Dickson.

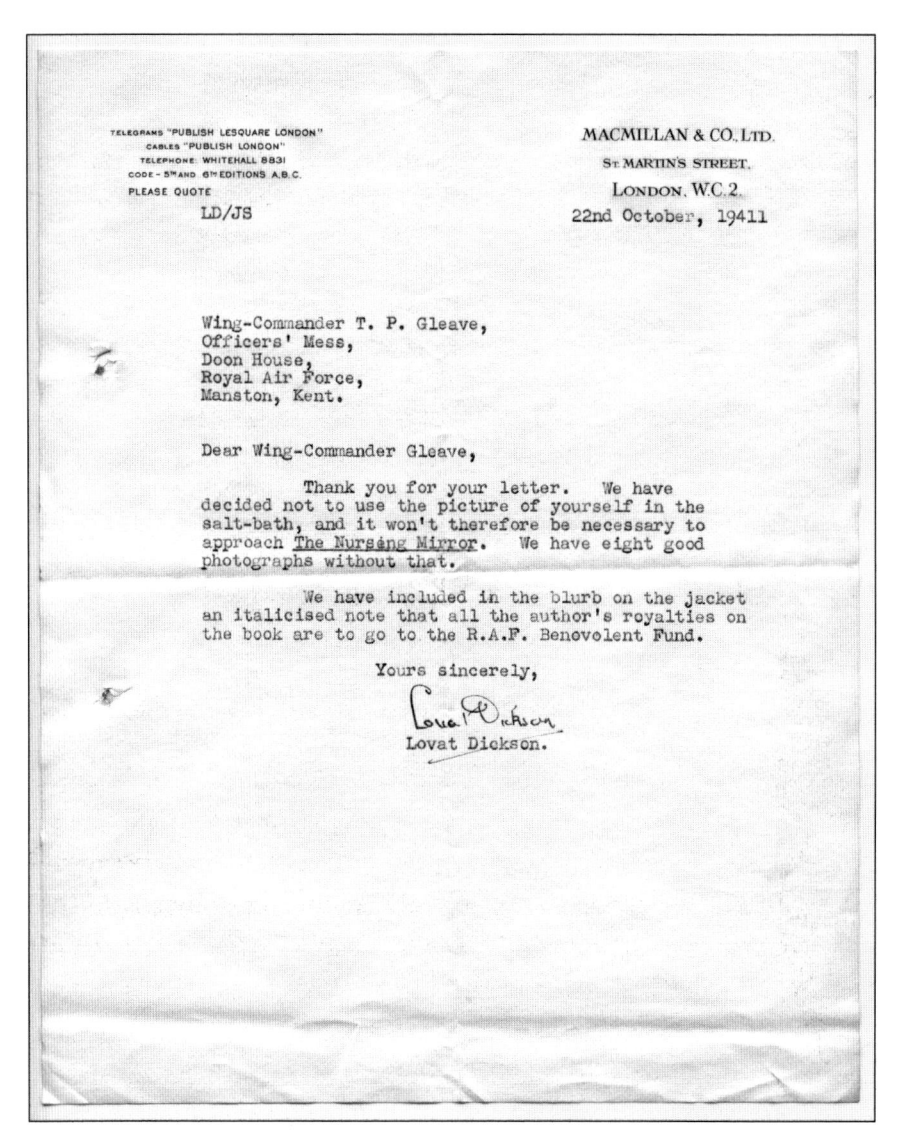

A letter from Lovat Dickson, which, dated 22 October 1941, includes a brief discussion on some of the proposed images that were to be used in the book.

THE JOURNEY TO PUBLICATION

```
TELEGRAMS "PUBLISH LESQUARE LONDON"              MACMILLAN & CO., LTD.
CABLES "PUBLISH LONDON"                          ST MARTIN'S STREET,
TELEPHONE WHITEHALL 8831
CODE - 5TH AND 6TH EDITIONS A.B.C.               LONDON, W.C.2.
PLEASE QUOTE   LD/VP

                                              8th December, 1941.


      Wing Commander T.P. Gleave,
      Officer's Mess,
      Royal Air Force,
      Manston, Kent.


      Dear Wing-Commander Gleave,

              Thank you for your letter. Some time had
      elapsed between my letter of the 11th November and your
      answer to it of December 6th. Meanwhile, the book has
      become ready for publication, and we are to publish it on
      December 12th - four days hence. Your six author's copies
      are going to you under separate cover today. Would you
      let us know what you wish to do in regard to the five
      hundred copies you said originally you intended to purchase ?
      If this arrangement could be left until after Christmas, it
      would, I think, be of advantage to the book since it would
      enable us to hold the stock of our present edition against
      any unforeseen demands that are likely to arise between
      publication and Christmas-time.

              I am afraid that paper regulations, which are
      very strict, prevent the insertion of any loose material in
      a book. We could not, therefore, use the cartoon as an
      insert. The prospectus will be printed on quite good paper,
      and the cartoon can be easily cut away and framed by anyone
      who might desire to do so.

              I am afraid that we have overlooked the page which
      you say is to contain messages of good wishes, although I
      remember you spoke of this originally. But so much time has
      elapsed that it has slipped my mind. Was it your intention
      that this page should go in the prospectus, or did you mean
      it to go in the book ? It is, of course, too late for the
      latter; and it would be an unusual addition to a prospectus
      for a volume which we hope will be able to stand on its own
      feet, and will interest the public by the merits of its
      story alone.

                                           Yours sincerely,

                                           Lovat Dickson.
```

Lovat Dickson wrote to Tom Gleave on 8 December 1941 with the news that his book was finally due for release on 12 December.

The dust jacket of the first edition of *I Had a Row With a German*, which went on sale on in the middle of December 1941.

PART II

I HAD A ROW WITH A GERMAN
A Battle of Britain Casualty

by
'R.A.F. Casualty'

I HAD A ROW WITH A GERMAN

Cuthbert Orde's portrait of Squadron Leader (later Group Captain) Tom Gleave, which was drawn on 21 September 1941.

Foreword

by Air Vice-Marshal Leigh-Mallory

It is a privilege to contribute a foreword to this modest story of gallantry and fortitude, told by a Fighter Pilot who fought and was badly wounded in the Battle of Britain.

I commend this book to the great British Public, who owe so much to those gallant gentlemen – the Fighter Pilots of the Royal Air Force.

T. Leigh-Mallory
Air Vice-Marshal
Uxbridge, 10 August 1941

Preface

This book forms a narrative of events that took place immediately prior to and subsequent to the Declaration of War, September 3rd, 1939.

Some are events which affected everyone: some which affected a few: some which are only of personal import. In recording the latter, I have displayed personal feeling, perhaps personal opinions, but I am not known to you and it therefore matters little.

If, however, there are some omissions or chronological disorders which might appear to the reader, I humbly apologise for them.

I have tried to be as accurate as memory permits, but there are events that live as yesterday, yet I can give them no place; faces I know as I do my kin, yet I cannot name them.

The Author

Chapter 1

I Make a Vow

I stepped off the train at a deserted village station on the West Coast of Scotland. It was raining hard, low clouds draped the surrounding hills, and the gathering darkness added its contribution to misery already felt.

I had been on three days' leave and had spent it with my wife and son. They were staying with my people further south, and it wasn't very healthy there at night; I hated leaving them; that depressed me, but the journey back depressed me still more. Trains are nauseating to those who fly, even fast trains: this one had started, stopped, changed coaches, started again for a while, then repeated the process. There was a war on, and I suppose I was lucky to get a train, but I had a bee in my bonnet and it stung. I had sat for hours in that train going over the events of twelve months before, and the more I thought the harder the darned bee stung …

August 1939, a few days before the now famous Sunday, I was on annual leave. My wife and I and our small son had decided to alter the surface of Bognor beach with a small wooden spade and bucket, for the benefit of my son. Tea was to be provided; the weather was ideal for picnics, everything was set. I was just going out to start the car when the 'phone rang, as 'phones do on such occasions. I turned back and lifted up the receiver.

"Report back immediately," came a voice from the other end of the line. It was Roger.

"Sorry," he said; and so was I.

He rang off, and I prepared to change, pack, and push off. I said goodbye to the family; we were staying at my in-law's house on the South Coast, and in two hours' time I was at my appointed place on duty.

I was told to get moving: someone was drawing a bead on someone else. He had done it before, but this time something had to be done about it.

I had been in the Service ten years, the last seven of which had been overshadowed by 'The Expansion'. The minds of all the Services had been dominated during this time by one question, 'What is Germany going to do?' They had been by no means alone in this respect; the man-in-the-street was thinking along the same lines. Like most people, I had read many articles on the subject, and books by the dozen. I remembered one in particular: not a book of direct prophecy or of suggestion, but a compilation of contemporary facts from which the smallest mind could glean things of future portent. Its name was *Insanity Fair*.

I collected my instruments and, together with Frank, head of our branch, and Roger, I drove over to Fighter Command Headquarters. It was here that we were to work and have our being during this time of war.

Next evening, I was off duty for twenty-four hours, and I drove over to Iver. The family was back in the cottage where we had spent seven happy months; now we were talking of packing, storing.

I stayed with them that night, and next day we packed, handed over the cottage and parted. I drove back to Fighter Command Headquarters, sad at heart. I felt sorry for those who would soon have to do the same, some for the second time in a lifetime. I thought of my parents; they had had their share of war and had known, what was worse, the aftermath. Now the few years that might still be theirs to spend in peace and security, a fitting end to lives honourably lived, were to be darkened, perhaps ended. I thought of millions like them. I thought of my wife and son going south – I swore that somehow,

I MAKE A VOW

I would do my humble share to rid the earth of one German, even if it cost me my neck. I should then at least have been of some use to humanity. I made that vow.

In the Holy of Holies, Operations Fighter Command Headquarters, I worked by day and sometimes by night. On September 3rd, 1939, I heard the solemn words of a broken-hearted old man. History was being made, but the fact did not register with me; there were more personal thoughts running through my mind, as they were running through millions of minds.

The actual declaration of war affected us little if at all. The whole machinery of war was already functioning; Commands, Groups, and Stations were at the ready. Perhaps in the more sober times to come honour will be paid to those who planned and organised, often working far into the long hours of the night that this might be so. I was of little importance, but I knew some of those who did the work; what they had was used to the full, what they had not was no fault of theirs.

I liked my job; it was interesting and responsible. The Branch were a grand lot, and so were the rest of the Operational Staff. But I longed for a flying job. I wanted to be back on fighters. I loved them and had flown little else but fighters and fighter-trainers for two thousand or more hours. I had no wish to do otherwise.

The months went by. Many times, I saw the Hun plotted on the table, saw the fighters plotted as they went up to blast him out of the skies, and heard the result coming over the 'phone. The sight of a Hun plot made my right thumb itch. I saw the Bomber Boys plotted out on long and difficult missions; I saw them return. Sometimes they did not all return; 'flak' or weather took occasional toll. There could be none who saw these continuous nightly, sometimes daily, treks to various parts of the Continent without feeling the greatest admiration for the pilots and crews of the bombers.

It was part of our allotted task to set the machinery of the Rescue Services in motion when any of our bombers were in trouble over the sea. This task was given all the attention we could devote to it. We constantly sought improvements, submitted suggestions, and always found a ready response. These rescue services have now been improved still further. At their head there is a Director, and additional facilities have been placed at his disposal. Rescue launches have been increased in numbers and improved in many ways. No efforts were spared, and none have since been spared, to make the combined work of the rescue services more efficient and more effective.

Fighters and aircraft of other Commands also benefit from these facilities, not forgetting the occasional Hun. We were instrumental in saving the crew of at least one Hun bomber shot down in the North Sea whilst attacking some of our shipping. Another part of our task was to aid bombers trying to reach their bases in bad weather. As time passed, we were able to improve this service too and, with the help of the Observer Corps, now the Royal Observer Corps – an honour well deserved – we were able to help many a bomber pilot and crew on their homeward journey.

When I could get away, I would visit the local aerodrome. There was a Station Flight there, made up of training and communication aircraft. What I usually did was to borrow one of these machines and push off to a Fighter or Bomber Station for an hour or two: it was always a tonic to meet those who were doing the real work. Sometimes I amused myself with half an hour's aerobatics on a Magister, or a little 'flap' investigation on a Mentor.

Geoff, one of the members of our Branch, would sometimes come and 'dice with death' in a dog-fight. He was a fine pilot, one of the few who held a Master Instructor's ticket. I enjoyed those spells; they gave me a chance to let off steam. The General, as he was called, ran the Flight and I found in him a friend in need, for rarely was I unable to get hold of an aircraft of some description and occasionally I got a Hind Trainer: it was good. It was even better when I managed to borrow a Gladiator, but this only happened very occasionally as other pilots in the same boat as myself had the same idea as I had.

I MAKE A VOW

When the weather was unfavourable for flying, I spent some of my spare time in the Drawing Office at Headquarters. I loved designing and inventing things; it always had fascinated me, and still does. As a side line I acted as president of a subsidiary mess where I lived during my enforced separation from the family. There was plenty of work attached to this job – finding new accommodation for additional members, problems of staff, etc. – and I found the remainder of my spare time fully occupied. It was, however, good to be employed: it kept my mind busy and I think I really enjoyed it, especially the mess parties we arranged as an antidote to the monotony of routine. I made many friends whilst living in that mess, members of all three Fighting Services. Some were regulars, others came from diverse walks of life. There was a famous K.C., a well-known singer, a skier of Olympic fame, several gentlemen from Fleet Street, and many others. It is good to recall the pleasure of their company.

One day I heard talk of vacancies – Squadron Leaders were wanted. I had waited months for this opportunity, and here it was at last. I had a chat with Frank, who was head of the Branch; he had no objection. The Volunteer Reserve members were all trained and fit to take over from me. I went to the Group Captain's office. He was in and willing to see me; he was grand. I saw the Air Vice-Marshal; he was grand too. Everything was grand. It would all be fixed, all be arranged.

True to their word, I had not long to wait. I pushed off on a few days' leave, to be recalled when required. I borrowed a Magister and flew down to the South Coast to be with my family again. Nearby was a Fighter Station which I knew well – I had spent happy times there years before – and there I parked the aircraft. Squadron Leader 'W' at Headquarters had already arranged for me to do some flying with one of the Squadrons stationed there: his son was also in the R.A.F. at an aerodrome in the neighbourhood and I had promised to look him up. By a coincidence, just after I arrived, I was asked to collect a pilot who was stranded somewhere on the South-East Coast; it turned out to be his son. I have since heard that he has been killed.

Dusty commanded the Squadron with whom I was to fly. He was an old friend of mine and I knew he would fix up something for me; he did. He lent me a Master and I spent two days instructing a new pilot. I enjoyed that; I liked the Master, and felt that no longer was I in danger of becoming out-of-date, a fear I had secretly nursed.

The Dunkirk show was on. Hurricanes were landing and taking off incessantly. I saw them come; I saw them go; some didn't return. I saw the pilots step out of their 'planes and gather on the tarmac, weary-eyed, tired, 'flaked-out': a brief rest, then off again. Dusty was tired and terribly worried; he knew just what was being asked of his pilots. I yearned to go with them, to give just one man a break; I admired them all beyond words. I had a feeling of shame when I talked to them; they were going through hell while I was enjoying myself. I asked Dusty if I could go over with them; he said he would fix something up for me when I had flown a Hurricane for a bit; perhaps I could lead a Section.

If I could have had just one trip over Dunkirk, I would have been happy; I would have been conscious of having given someone a rest, a rest deserved as no one has ever deserved one before. But that was not to be. A signal arrived; I was to report to a Fighter Station in Lincolnshire. I had been attached to a Hurricane Squadron to bring myself up to date as a modern fighter pilot.

I bade farewell to Dusty and the Station C.O.; they had been good to me and I was very grateful. After a short leave, I climbed into the Magister and was off. I spent the night at Fighter Command, and in the morning packed my kit into the car and started off for Lincolnshire.

The Squadron I was to be attached to was re-forming. It had been split up to augment other Squadrons which had suffered casualties during the invasion of the Low Countries, and was now receiving new pilots from Training Units and from other Squadrons. A few of the original pilots remained; their old C.O. was missing, believed killed, and the new one had the job of welding the Squadron together.

I MAKE A VOW

I had met him some years before, but had not had time to get to know him. Now that I had the chance, I found him a great help.

Life on the Station was good. The officers were keen and full of zest, and so were the N.C.O.s and troops. They were well looked after and plenty of entertainment was provided. Everybody was well fed, and the best was made of available accommodation. Although uncompleted it was a model Station, and little wonder; there could be few better Station Commanders. He created a bond of sympathy between the ground staff and the pilots, for whom after all the Station really existed, a fact which no one was allowed to forget. I loved that Station and everything on it; I only needed my family to be nearer, and a few minutes with a Hun, to make life complete.

I spent a fortnight flying on every possible occasion; the weather was perfect, so were the Hurricanes. Things had altered a lot since I was last in a Fighter Squadron, not so much in principle as in detail. I found plenty of things to do and plenty of new ideas to get 'buttoned up'. I was finding my feet again and felt better for it.

I dropped a Hurricane one day and might have broken a less robust aircraft. I felt ashamed of myself; I still had a lot to learn. Gone were the days of biplane daisy-cutting, the age of flying umbrellas. I got to know the Hurricane like a book, it was the grandest thing I had ever flown: treated right and properly handled it was 'Pilot's Delight'.

One evening I was sitting in the mess, talking shop with some of the Squadron, when the Squadron C.O. came in. He was in a hurry; he had been promoted and appointed to command a new Station up North, and I was to take over the Squadron. It was grand news for me; I felt like 'letting my hair down', as Jack, one of the Squadron, always described a night out.

The Squadron had to be re-formed, trained, and put on the top line in the shortest possible time. It was the sort of job I revelled in, for one could get results and see them: some jobs never seem to produce anything but sweat and tears.

I HAD A ROW WITH A GERMAN

I knew most of the Squadron by now: what experience they had had and what they could do.

Bill was my Senior Flight Commander. He had spent his time in a ground job before joining the Squadron, and now, back on flying again, his enthusiasm knew no bounds: he was dying to pump lead into a Hun – we had much in common.

Bruno, my other Flight Commander, was no less enthusiastic. He had fought over Dunkirk with another Squadron and had been shot down over there, but he had managed to get back safely.

Bill's Flight included the following:

'The Colonel': He was deputy Flight Commander. I had known him when a pupil, and found he was still gifted with a great sense of humour.

'Newly Married': A recent arrival, originally with the Fleet Air Arm and now converting to fighters.

'Jenks': Put up a fine show in France.

'Bell-Pusher': He did likewise. He was also the owner of a small and very much open Austin Seven, and periodically held 'Gladiatorial' ramming contests with another car of similar make from the other Flight. The aerodrome formed the arena, and on quiet days it was safer to sit in a bell tent than outside 'within combat range'.

'Dopey' and 'Dimmy': Two new arrivals from a Training Unit who were inseparable: their nicknames were no reflection on their mental ability.

'Air Commodore Handlebars': A Canadian who had just arrived. He had formerly been on bombers and was now converting to fighters. His nickname evolved through the constant attention paid to his moustache – a real roadster model.

'Sammy' and 'Nohow': Two Polish pilots who were great assets to the Squadron and liked by all.

Of the sergeant pilots, two were old hands, one having fought in France and the other over Dunkirk. Two others had recently arrived from Training Units and Bill took them under his wing, together with

I MAKE A VOW

Dopey and Dimmy, and soon had them as full of offensive spirit as himself.

Bruno's Flight were all old hands with the exception of three sergeant pilots who were recent arrivals but practically fully trained, and they were as follows:

'Jack': He was deputy Flight Commander: A New Zealander who had already met the Hun in France and knew what to do with him.

'Curly': He was another who had no doubts about his job. He owned the other Austin Seven.

'The Group Captain': An ultra-efficient young officer who had done well both in France and over here. His very correct manner earned for him this austere title.

'Percy': Another experienced Hun-blaster. He should have been called 'Smiler', for nothing seemed to disturb his outlook on life, it was always humorous.

'Corky': He was renowned for his ready wit and also for his artistic talents. He was always prepared for the worst, and when it happened, he would remark, "I suppose it is for the best." He too had already met the Hun and knew his measure.

I spent the next few days in the office with 'Cap', the Squadron Adjutant, reorganising the Flights and Sections. I toured the barrack blocks; they were well organised, thanks to my disciplinarian, an old hand who had come back to do his bit, as do all the right kind. Things went smoothly, much smoother than I thought possible. I discussed problems with Bill and Bruno; we found the answers, and things went still more smoothly. The pilots' training chart began to fill; it was filled daily. Bill was in charge of the training, and no abler fellow ever took on a job of that kind. Occasionally we would all gather for an argument, a lecture, anything useful. I always told them why I wanted a thing done, and I was never let down.

On some evenings, just before dusk when work was finished until dawn next day, we played soccer with a ball kindly presented by the Comforts Fund. Sides would be chosen, usually inter-Flight, and the

I HAD A ROW WITH A GERMAN

maximum amount of clothing would be discarded compatible with the requirements of a quick take-off. Among the fitters and riggers was some promising talent, and they led us a dance. I usually joined Bill's team, but nevertheless I occasionally got in the way of one of his famous runs, on which he would be furiously backed by 'The Colonel' and one of his sergeant pilots, and neither friend nor foe found it healthy for their shins.

During this time, we held part of the Squadron, the old hands, ready for operational purposes. When I had time, I would stand by with a Section or Flight, much to the disgust of Bruno and Bill who regarded my activities as a definite attempt to poach the first Hun; nor were they far wrong.

Another Squadron shared the aerodrome with us. It was a Spitfire Squadron and was commanded by Tubby, whom I had known for a long time. He was an excellent fellow to work with, and so was his Squadron; their co-operation did much to make my job easier and much to make the life of my Squadron a pleasant one, both in the mess and in the air.

We made progress. We started Squadron formation in earnest, sometimes close, sometimes open, and finally in battle array. It was a grand sight from the leader's viewpoint. We usually flew as three Sections; each Section being composed of two pairs of aircraft. The pilot on the exposed side of each sub-formation kept watch, weaving along the flank. Sometimes, on cloudy days, one Section went above a layer of cloud while the rest would fly below; occasionally positions were reversed and, as time passed, we were able to fly well dispersed but never out of touch with the leading Section. This practice proved invaluable later. We practised fighter attacks in Squadron, Flight, and Section formations until we were well-nigh perfect. We soon became fully operational by day, doing our full share of the daily watch.

We passed on to Wing formation. Tubby would lead with his Squadron and we would formate on him. It was not easy at first, but we improved on each occasion, and were soon able to operate with precision.

Despite the paper-work and other matters which required one's presence in the office, I was able to do plenty of flying. My log included training, ferrying, and gun-laying, i.e., acting as target for the gunners, which was always good fun, in addition to Operational flights which formed the majority. These latter were varied, sometimes an order to 'Patrol coastline, etc.', or 'Patrol convoy' – skating about over the North Sea, looking for Huns bent on attacking shipping, and occasionally passing a salute to a friendly Hudson, the 'tireless eyes' of convoy escort – or perhaps 'Patrol base' followed by an attempt to intercept; but the Huns rarely came near in daytime.

Only on one occasion did I see a Hun by day while I was up North. I had been standing by for night flying and, after a quiet night, had lain down on a camp bed, one of several we kept in the pilots' marquee. A bell rang in the bell-tent where the Operations orderly kept watch. He came rushing into the marquee.

"You are to patrol base at 2,000 ft., sir," he said. "Operations have just been on."

I jumped up, put on my flying kit and parachute, and ran to my machine. Jenks, who was standing by with me, was already beside his machine, and both aircraft were running up. We climbed in, turned to avoid parked aircraft, and opened up. It was now quite light, no wind and a clear sky; a perfect dawn. We climbed rapidly and soon reached our height; we were then told to climb to 20,000 ft. on a certain vector. I set course and we climbed as fast as we could go. Jenks was on my right, two or three spans out. I could see him searching ahead and to his flank, sometimes turning out slightly to search aft; he knew his stuff. I searched ahead and to the left. We were approaching our height. I turned on a bit more oxygen, glanced round the cockpit and eyed the firing button: all was set.

Then came the voice from Operations over the radio telephone, "Aircraft approaching you from the east." Jenks heard it too. He went up a bit and fell back to cover my tail. "Aircraft now close to you," blurted the radio telephone. I searched right, left, and centre, but I could see nothing. I strained my head back and, right above, I saw a glint, another further on, then another. It was a Hun reconnaissance machine: it must have been at 35,000 ft. if a foot. I turned west and started to climb but I lost him; he was not intent on loitering. We returned, disappointed, to the aerodrome, feeling like people who had been cheated at cards. On paper it was a perfect interception as regards course and speed, but height had beaten us. The Operations people had done their job well. Height was always a problem: the Huns were no better off over this.

Enemy aircraft were coming over at night in small numbers during that period, usually on a wide front. We had a spell of good weather and managed to get in a fair measure of night-flying training between dusk and 'Warning Red', which meant grounding those under instruction. We had four trained night pilots, Bill, Bruno, one of our sergeant pilots who was an old hand, and myself. We took it in turns to stand by when Huns were over, and had some good trips on occasions, but never struck oil. I took a bead on an aircraft one moonlight night, turned the button to 'fire' but luckily withheld it – it was Bruno. He had seen something and was going hell-for-leather after it, but lost it.

I learnt a lot about night flying on modern types during those nights. I had done quite a bit on Hart Variants and Hinds, but found the conceptions I hitherto held had vastly changed. Waffling down through the mirk, feeling your way on wings of lesser load, were things of the past; you either had 'lift' and plenty of it, or 'flowers'. I learnt that one night with a vengeance. Tubby had warned me of running into pea-soup and of skating about in the blackout. It was not like peace-time night flying; different to the nights when I used to take pupils to see the lights of Blackpool. I had taken off to patrol along a line on the coast; it was slightly hazy but fine, and a few stars were visible.

I MAKE A VOW

Near the coast there was a layer of cloud about 10,000 ft. up, and I patrolled just above it. It was clear up there, and as my eyes became accustomed to the dark, I found I could see a comfortable distance ahead. I flew for an hour or so, and was then recalled. I put the nose down and set course for base, having been given a vector home. I entered the cloud layer and held course, keeping the rate of descent constant. After a few minutes, when I reckoned I should be clear of cloud, I looked out of 'the office'; it was black, black as Indian ink. I received another vector and reset course, still losing height – 5,000 ft. – 3,000 ft. – 1,000 ft. I could see nothing.

At 500 ft. I levelled out, held a brief one-man conference, and rang up home. They gave me another vector, so I thought; actually, it was for someone else. I set course, climbed up a bit, and then heard Operations calling me. They gave me a fresh vector and I turned, set course and flew back, glancing out of the 'office' now and then as I approached what I thought would be the locality of the aerodrome. I could see nothing. I called up Operations and they gave me my position together with a fresh vector; the aerodrome was apparently on my left and ahead of me.

Operations informed me that the searchlight was about to be switched on, and a few seconds later I saw its welcome beam, turned to dull orange by the thick haze. I landed; having learnt something no book could ever teach me. The clouds had closed up, the haze had thickened, and I had come down expecting to see at least a beacon if not the dull outline of the flare-path. I must have been almost over the aerodrome twice, but had not yet learnt to appreciate the distance a modern aircraft, with a high minimum safe flying speed, can cover in a turn on instruments: nor the precious little time there is to take one's eyes off the instruments, glance outside the 'office' and then glue them to the instrument board again before the needles go haywire. Stability is not a virtue with single-engined fighters, whatever their breed.

Two pilots in Tubby's Squadron got a Hun each while we were there. One pilot crashed, however, having been hit by the Hun during

I HAD A ROW WITH A GERMAN

the scrap. He injured his back, but I heard he would be all right eventually; it was tough luck after putting up such a good show. Tubby was believed to have got one, but did not claim it; an aircraft was heard to have crashed in the Humber, but confirmation was difficult.

I saw a Hun only once at night the whole time I was there. It was full moon and a glorious night. I was sent up to 18,000 ft. to patrol near the coast. I could see Ack-Ack fire a few miles to the north, and searchlights weaving about. I had turned to fly to the north end of the line when Operations gave me a vector east. I altered my course and flew towards a bank of cloud just seaward of the coast. I was expecting to see a Hun, if any, come sneaking in over the top or just beneath.

Suddenly a green and a white light appeared from out of the cloud a mile or so away; the white light disappeared almost immediately, and the green light moved quickly to the right and vanished in the cloud. I raced after it, but saw nothing further. I found afterwards that there had been a Hun there, and I can only surmise that he had navigation lights on to cheat the gunners. That I saw no red port light or white tail light is still a mystery to me. The fact remained, however, that I had been done out of a chance to perforate a Hun, and I returned feeling there was little justice in the world.

On another occasion I completely 'bought a pup'. I had to laugh, although inwardly annoyed. The sky was partially covered by several layers of very much broken cloud: on the ground there was a fair amount of light, but above the clouds, about 15,000 ft., it was bright moonlight, a grand night to be up. I patrolled for a while at this height and was then instructed by Operations to come lower. A few Huns were coming in near the mouth of the Humber, and I flew north in the hope of meeting one of them. Suddenly I saw a black object through a gap in the clouds; it was straight ahead of me and appeared to be travelling in the same direction. I opened up to maximum boost and rapidly overhauled the object. It increased in size until its shape became grotesque.

I MAKE A VOW

Against a light background of moonlit cloud, it appeared perfectly round with a miniature 'tailplane and rudder' protruding above and from the sides respectively. As I flew through the cloud-gap and emerged into a clear area I realised the object was stationary. I was closing distance at the rate of knots, wondering what it could be. Then, as I saw the tailplane and rudder appear to thicken and assume the shape of lobes, I realised it was a barrage balloon. I pulled up and turned, beating a hasty retreat as I gained height. Other balloons appeared to the right and to the left of me as I climbed, but luckily, I was above them. A balloon barrage is no place for loitering; most unhealthy in fact.

Only once was I forced to land away from my base at night. I was up with another Hurricane, and we were patrolling at different heights over the coast above cloud. Nothing came our way, and after about an hour's flying, I heard Operations directing the other pilot south. A few minutes later I received similar orders and set course accordingly. As I flew south the clouds thinned and finally disappeared, revealing a blanket of fog stretching as far as the eye could see.

After some minutes' flying time I came to a clear patch and saw an aerodrome I knew well. Operations had been accurate to a degree in their plotting, and I landed as dawn was breaking. The other pilot was already down, and we pushed off to the mess to enjoy a welcome plate of bacon and eggs. Our hosts were most hospitable, and we much appreciated their efforts to make us feel at home. I knew that Geoff was now stationed there, and later, at a more reasonable hour, I went along to his room and knocked on his door. A very tired voice told me to "Come in."

I entered and saw Geoff, looking like death, slowly raising himself up in bed, his efforts being made with much guttural accompaniment. He told me that he had retired early the night before, feeling 'flaked out' and with a splitting headache. He was doing a responsible Operations job most successfully, but was not looking the same man as when I knew him as a pilot. Recently I heard he was back on a

Chief Flying Instructor's job, a post he filled in civil life for twenty-odd years and in which he became known as a master. I bet he looks a different man now.

I said goodbye to Geoff and was sorry I had disturbed him, good though it was to see him again, and then returned to the mess. A message came through to say our base was now clear of fog, so, together with my fellow pilot, I pushed off for home.

I enjoyed these nocturnal trips and much regretted that we drew a blank. Huns were fewer on those nights, but certainly more adventurous than they were by day. We were all equally anxious to see the first Hun fall since the Squadron re-formed. Pilots and crews, technicians, clerks, aircraft hands, all were dying for 'the bag'. It was always a great encouragement to the pilots to see the enthusiasm displayed by the ground personnel, and I often regret that their gallant, indispensable, and vital existence is often overshadowed in the minds of many by the more glamourous doings of those who fly. In no less a way does this apply to the non-flying officers of a Squadron: there is no glamour for them but they are equally indispensable, and few things pleased me more than the grand way the pilots of the Squadron treated Cap, my Adjutant, and Henry, the Intelligence Officer: they were always made to feel full members of the team, as they undoubtedly were.

Then we suffered our first casualty. He was a sergeant pilot who had taken off, just after dawn, accompanying Bill to intercept a raider approaching from the North Sea. A cloud layer extended from about 2,000 ft. to 11,000 ft., and they had climbed up through it in search of the Hun. There were gaps in the layer higher up, and Bill and the sergeant became separated as they altered course directed by Operations. Bill eventually returned; the Hun having headed back for the safety of the open sea. The sergeant was missing, and shortly afterwards we heard that an aircraft had crashed near the coast. I took off to investigate, and when I reached the locality, I ran into a heavy rainstorm.

I MAKE A VOW

Visibility was low, and I had much difficulty in keeping a level course while searching the area at the same time. I found no trace of the aircraft, however, and returned to the aerodrome. Later a search party discovered the wreckage and found the sergeant dead. We could only surmise that, in following Bill and keeping watch through gap and cloud, he had inadvertently lost control. The conditions below were such as to make recovery extremely difficult, and he had crashed. He was a very decent and acceptable member of the team, and we were sorry to lose him.

One day I was instructed by the Station C.O. to take forty-eight hours' leave; I was to push off that night. I always enjoyed my leave twofold when told to take it; I never felt then that I was neglecting my job or that I might miss the chance of a Hun through my own personal arrangements had I requested leave. My family had now moved north and were staying on the Lancashire coast with my parents, and I set off cross-country to visit them.

It was good to see them; good to see my people again after many months.

Next morning, I was up, but not very early; I was enjoying this leave thoroughly. Towards noon my wife and I and our small son went down to the beach. It was a lovely day and we could see the Welsh mountains a long way off to the west, cutting a jagged pattern against the distant sky. I remembered the many happy hours I had spent flying over that lovely scene years before when I flew on an 'A' licence from a Merseyside aerodrome, and later, in the Service, when I was stationed on Deeside. I remembered too the happy days I had spent as a small boy touring through North Wales with my people on those greatest of all schoolboy occasions, the holidays.

To the north-west stretched Liverpool Bay, green seas haunted by memories of silver sails and majestic ships of bygone days. I could still remember how I used to stand on that same spot during the last war watching the great liners come steaming in, grotesque in their coat of war paint – *Olympic, Aquitania,* and that grand old lady of the seas, *Mauretania.*

To the south-west I could see the Wirral. To the south a noble river wound its way through a maze of shipping, and on its eastern bank, beneath a canopy of haze slashed here and there by columns of different-coloured smoke, could be seen the dark grey outline of a great city. It was there that I saw my first dawn; there where I lived and grew up.

"It's nearly lunch-time," I heard my wife calling, putting an end to my musings. I rose to my feet, persuaded my young son to abandon his sandy fortress, and we set off for home.

Lunch was not quite ready when we returned, and I sat down to glance through the daily paper. The 'phone rang, and I answered the call. Once again, I heard that familiar command, "Come back immediately."

The playful tune of a telephone bell is no longer music to me; I have other views.

I rammed my kit into a small suitcase, said goodbye all round, and started off.

I arrived back at the aerodrome that evening in time to see Cap, the Adjutant, before he packed up for the day. He was working late and, as I entered the office which we shared, he looked up from his desk, piled high with files and loose printed matter, and said, "The Squadron moves to-morrow. We are to go north and the move is to be completed as early in the day as possible."

Cap had already settled many details and, after a short discussion, we walked over to the mess. Bill and Bruno were there, and we were able to complete final arrangements. I had a long talk with the Station C.O. He was genuinely sorry we were going and so was the Squadron; it was a hard break after the excellent treatment we had received from everyone there and it had been sheer pleasure to work with them.

We had supper, and afterwards joined the 'concert party' in the ante-room. This was to be our last night here, and we were bent on

I MAKE A VOW

making the best of it. Peter, whom I had known at Fighter Command Headquarters, had recently arrived as an Operations officer. He had been right through the French show and had many vivid tales to tell of his escape, but unfortunately, we were to part again after all too brief a reunion – another regret I had to add to the many already held on leaving. Peter joined the party; it was like old times in the pre-blitz days. After a lengthy session – towards the end of which voices began to flag, new songs became scarce, and serious attempts at singing turned to humorous efforts – we broke up and pushed off to bed.

The following morning was one of great activity. Aircraft were serviced and details issued to pilots. The ground staff packed their goods and chattels into lorries and headed north, a nucleus of essential personnel remaining behind to await Air Transport. 'The Colonel' had gone ahead the previous evening to prepare for our arrival, and I rang through to warn him that all was set and when to expect us. We had an early lunch, and shortly afterwards the Air Transport arrived. Light equipment and kit were weighed and packed in, personnel embarked, and the aerial convoy took off for its destination. In a few minutes we were off the ground, rapidly forming up as we set course for our new base.

The weather was not up to the standard of the past few weeks, but was nevertheless quite pleasant. Occasionally we altered course to avoid a local rainstorm; at other times we flew in brilliant sunshine as we passed beneath a break in the cloud. Further north we found the hills covered with cloud and edged towards the coast to skirt the slopes, and then, further on, when we again emerged into clear sky, we could see in the distance the shimmering outline of the Forth with the Scottish hills beyond. In a few minutes we had landed at our new base on the south bank of the estuary.

'The Colonel' greeted us and gave us our allotted positions. The Station C.O. was away for the day, so I remained with the Squadron at dispersal point until the aircraft had been sorted out and parked.

I HAD A ROW WITH A GERMAN

The Air Transport had arrived just before, and the last of the 'flying pantechnicons' – a converted old-time Harrow Bomber – was being unloaded. A few pilots and skeleton crews were detailed to stand by for any emergency, and the rest of us repaired to our various messes to get some tea. The evening was spent in checking up on meals and accommodation for our men, and the day's proceedings were wound up with a visit to our new Station Operations room, which, incidentally, was also Sector Control. Here I met Johnny, one of the three Operations officers with whom we were to become great friends.

We spent the next few days settling down in our new abode. We received our roster of duty, and those pilots who were not required for Operational flying reconnoitred the district, checking up on prominent landmarks and general topography.

During those few days I became aware of a little less enthusiasm amongst the men: they worked with a will, but not in the same gay spirit as hitherto. They were the grandest crowd one could wish to work with; I had never found it otherwise in the Service, and I took steps to find out what was worrying them. With the help of my Adjutant and Flight-sergeant disciplinarian the bogy was soon laid. It was food and accommodation. The food itself was good, very good, but the cooking was not up to standard, and meals were often cold: so far as accommodation was concerned, it was a question of providing the wherewithal that transforms a bare room into a habitable place.

Determined to let nothing cause the men any anxiety or discomfort, I called on the Station Adjutant and, with him, toured the kitchens and men's dining-room. The cause of the failure of the kitchens was obvious. Hundreds of men had passed through this Station within a few weeks, and even now there was a considerable number still on the camp awaiting movement orders; yet the kitchens, in fact the whole of the feeding facilities, were only originally designed for one Squadron. Work was proceeding as quickly as possible on new and more modern cook-houses, as well as on barrack blocks. It was no fault of the cooks nor those in authority; the requirements of war vastly outweigh those of peace, and the necessary changes cannot be effected overnight, nor can the Service prepare to meet them in times of peace if they have not the means.

Accommodation troubles were soon settled. Our men had moved into newly-built quarters and the furnishing equipment was already en route.

I explained the position to the troops, told them that meals would be improved, when possible, but warned them of the difficulties under which they were being fed. Once the position was known they accepted it philosophically and assumed that cheerful tone which had made them so popular elsewhere.

We were able to do a considerable amount of flying at our new Station, and took part in many hunts for Huns. By day, however, they kept at a respectful distance. At night a few came over at infrequent intervals. We volunteered to stand by with a few trained pilots, although officially we were not yet operational by night, and our offer was accepted. Night-flying training proceeded when conditions were favourable, but it was not so easy to arrange as it was at our previous base.

A mile or two to the north of us a balloon barrage flew to a considerable height; to the east and west were small hills or slag-heaps in close proximity to the aerodrome, and to the south the ground rose towards a range of hills some miles distant. Smoke haze frequently covered the area, and when it was thick landing became a tricky and sometimes a hazardous business. This obstacle precluded training on several nights and also interfered with Operational flying. I tried to get permission to operate from a near-by aerodrome where the local conditions were ideal for the job, but the Station C.O. would not agree to this. He gave me his views on the subject and I appreciated them, but I still felt that we were not getting maximum results. However, as the C.O. was preparing to leave for another post, I decided to await the arrival of the new C.O. before pursuing the question further.

I HAD A ROW WITH A GERMAN

The Squadron was now settling down well, and we longed for the chance of some real business. The new C.O. arrived and we made our number with him. I had known him before; he had flown a great deal and had sampled most modern types of aircraft. It was always a pleasure to lend him a 'plane when one could be spared, and his interest in both the flying and ground parts of our existence did much to gain for himself the respect and popularity of the whole Squadron. He readily agreed to our suggestions to improve both our day and night activities, thus enabling further progress to be made.

We were allowed to operate from the neighbouring aerodrome by night when conditions warranted this procedure, and it proved most successful. I myself enjoyed some good trips from there, and on one occasion, when my electrical equipment packed up, I was able to get down without difficulty, thanks to the excellent approaches to the landing area. It was possible to fly at a low level within a wide circle of the flare-path, an essential requirement for night flying in most weathers.

Every third night we were off duty. This meant a little relaxation in the local city, and the Squadron moved 'in convoy' to a prearranged rendezvous where the cares and woes of war were forgotten for a few happy hours. It also meant, incidentally, sleeping in a comfortable bed in the mess without fear of being disturbed from one's slumber, a pleasant thought to enhance the evening's entertainment.

I can remember several very enjoyable visits to that near-by city, and parties that remain in the memory, not only because I enjoyed them, but for something deeper than that. Practically every Allied nationality had been represented there, and it had been heartening to see many of those who have lost so much at the hands of the Hun finding a little happiness amongst their comrades of other lands, especially of our own, who treated them so well. Let us hope that in years to come we do all in our power to make these many temporary friendships and pleasant gatherings of different nationalities a permanent institution.

I MAKE A VOW

A fortnight passed: we had come to like this place and I, not the least, was enjoying the summer flying weather. Then one day I received notice of posting in the near future. A new C.O. had been appointed to command my Squadron, and I was to leave in a few days to take up the duties of an Acting Wing Commander at a new Group Headquarters. I felt that now I should never fulfil my vow; the last chance remained in the next two or three days, and it was decidedly slender.

'Star' arrived to take over; he had just relinquished command of a Flight in a Squadron stationed west of us, and was now overjoyed at receiving his first Squadron command. I had known him as a pupil and remembered him as a very charming fellow, efficient and full of the right Service ideas. I was glad that he was to take over the bunch of fine fellows I had had the honour to command; it was a deeply personal thing, and only those who have known what it is to command a Squadron or the like, under conditions of war, can appreciate the feelings I held. I handed over to Star, and spent the next couple of days helping him to find his feet. The Squadron took to him immediately; I found much consolation in that fact; human feelings count for much in a circle whose future is precarious to a greater or lesser degree.

The Air Officer Commanding our new Group visited the Station, and Star and I were interviewed by him. I had already learnt that I was to spend a few weeks at his Headquarters, prior to moving on to my new appointment, in order to learn something about Operations. As I had already acquired some knowledge of the subject, I pleaded with him to be allowed to stay with the Squadron during that period as I had not had the opportunity of meeting a Hun at close range. I had, incidentally, other reasons which were hard to express, and I let them slip out: I had constantly told the Squadron, especially the inexperienced ones, what we intended to do with the Hun when we found him and how we would do it; now I felt that I should be slipping off without the opportunity of showing them that I was willing to practise what I preached; it hurt my conscience.

I HAD A ROW WITH A GERMAN

The A.O.C. promised to talk to my future Group Commander, and in a short while I heard that I could remain with the Squadron. Star had already agreed to my doing this; in fact, he welcomed the idea, and life once again took on a rosy hue.

During the next week or so I spent much time in the air, and when Star was occupied with the affairs of administration in his office I stood by with the Squadron. Several times I undertook Convoy Patrol, and occasionally a sweep over the North Sea for possible prowling Huns, but none came our way. I had some good night trips, and altogether thoroughly enjoyed myself. Flying over the magnificent Scottish scenery was in itself a fine tonic, no doubt envied by many, even those who do not fly.

One day we were ordered to move to another base on the West Coast of Scotland: another Squadron was coming north for a rest and we were to replace a Squadron going south in its place. We were sorry to leave, having made many new friends. We were, however, still keeping contact with our old Station, who were in remote control of our new base as Sector Control so far as Operations were concerned, and this was some consolation for the move.

Next morning, at an early hour, I took off with half the Squadron and headed west. Star was remaining to see our ground personnel off and then bringing the rest of the Squadron with him.

We arrived at our new base in time to see the departing Squadron making final adjustments before setting off. I had known the C.O. when a pupil with him, so we had a chat about old times; then he was off. We refuelled, took up dispersal positions, and stood by in readiness. Star arrived just before lunch, and after arranging reliefs we pushed off together for the mess.

The Station C.O. greeted us and told us of the arrangements he had made. He had been in Civil Aviation before the war in charge of this aerodrome, which had been and still was a training centre. We found ourselves very well catered for; in fact, we lived in luxury whilst we were there, and the efforts of the Station C.O. to make our life pleasant were much appreciated. He threw a cocktail party for us to warm up our arrival, and it certainly did.

Star spent much time during the next few days checking up on accommodation and meals for the men, arranging the details of Operational requirements and various other matters. He asked me to take charge of the flying, and once again I was in my element. As a side line I occasionally acted as target for the local gunners, or tested aircraft after repair or major overhauls. Some evenings I spent wandering about the aerodrome enjoying the sunset. I remember the seemingly endless rows of Tiger Moths parked around the perimeter: in their top-coats of camouflage with yellow flanks and feet, shown to brighter shades by the rays of the setting sun, it was hard to believe that they were products of man's hands; they looked more like a host of feeding migrants.

Once or twice, as dusk was falling, I saw some new types of aircraft from the New World come sailing in to land, then off again into the gathering darkness. One I recognised as a Grumman Martlet, a pretty tubby little fighter with an attractive whine; another was the Brewster Buffalo of similar build but apparently more compact – it reminded me of the Gee Bee, a famous American racing aircraft of former days. It was good to see the sympathy of our American friends taking practical shape. Later, as night came on, I would sometimes visit a local hotel in company with some of the Squadron, and there enjoy an hour or two chatting to some of the Station staff who were billeted there.

One day I asked permission to take a small spot of leave so that I could be with my family again. I felt that any day now I should be whisked off north to my new job and would be further than ever away from them. My leave was granted, and off I shot to the local railway station. The journey down was tedious, but I did not care; I was willing to put up with anything so long as I reached home. Those few precious hours were heaven, and were gone before I had fully realised it. I was back on the train, heading north, and it seemed as though I had hardly left my carriage for more than a few minutes.

Now I was back at the Station near the aerodrome, after hours of brooding in the train, fully expecting to find my marching orders – my last chance would be gone to send some loathsome murderer to his end; I would have to say goodbye to the grandest bunch of chaps one could ever meet, and spend the rest of the war with my blood boiling uselessly in my veins.

That was why I felt miserable as I stepped off the train. I managed to get a taxi and drove to the mess, paid my chauffeur, and walked slowly up the steps to the entrance.

Chapter 2

The Black Cross

The mess was deserted. A low hum came from the radio set which someone had left on in the ante-room. I picked up an evening paper, lit a cigarette, and pressed the bar bell-push: a can of beer would be company. The barman came in wreathed in smiles, smiles prompted by anticipation of an order, however humble: it had been quiet in the mess that evening. My beer arrived in no time. He was a most efficient barman, but then the Service has always seemed blessed in that respect.

I switched the wireless off and settled down to read. The Blitz, better known now as the Battle of Britain, had slackened off; it was the indefinable end of what is now called the First Phase, but the papers still resounded to the echoes of its events. I put the paper down. It depressed me; it confirmed my opinion that I should miss the one last chance I still hoped for. Perhaps the Blitz was already being called off: our chaps had given the Hun a pasting, and he now had gaps in his teeth.

A bell rang on the mantelpiece; it was the field telephone from Squadron Operations room. A faint voice came over the wire; it was Johnny at Sector Control. The Squadron was to go south first thing to-morrow. I laughed.

"It's right," came Johnny's indignant reply. I nearly dropped the 'phone; I know I spilt some beer; it was unbelievable.

"You are wanted here, I think," came the voice. I felt like someone who had backed a winner at long odds and then seen the wretched thing disqualified.

I HAD A ROW WITH A GERMAN

"For God's sake do something about it, Johnny," I pleaded: and he must have done, for that was the last I was to hear about that. Johnny was one of the best.

I put the 'phone down and, with mixed feelings, pushed off to the mess call-box. I had to tell Star and the chaps. I asked the barman if he knew where they were and he suggested 'The Blossom', which was close by the aerodrome. I rang up, asked for Star, and waited. I heard his footsteps as he came to the other end of the line.

"You are going south," I blurted out, and I heard him laugh.

"No joking," I said; "it's true." His 'phone slammed down like a ton of bricks, and I had hardly settled down again to drain my can of beer when the rending of rubber tread, the scattering of gravel, and the screech of brakes filled my ears. They had arrived; they would awaken the dead; they nearly did!

"Who started this story?" asked someone as they trooped in.

"I did," I replied. "You're off to-morrow as soon as you can get going."

"How about you?" asked Bill. "You're coming too, aren't you?"

I told him about my conversation with Sector Control.

"Get going before they grab you, sir," he advised.

I had already decided to do that and asked Star if he had any objection. "No, of course not, you must certainly come," he replied. "You can take half of the Squadron down to-morrow, and push off as soon as you like." How I liked that fellow!

This was an occasion befitting a celebration. We must have the Flight-sergeants and sergeants in for a mess 'scrum'; they were a part of the team, and great fellows. Someone went for them and they did not need asking twice. Even the senior Flight-sergeant seemed rejuvenated, he was beaming like a satisfied broker as he came in. The mess was cleared of all breakables, pictures were stowed away in a place of safety, and drinks were handed round. Someone produced an old cushion and it was promptly tied up to simulate a rugger ball. It was to be Officers versus Sergeants, and the teams, divesting themselves of tunics and collars, rolled up their sleeves and scrummed down. I had taken the precaution of nipping back to my room and putting on the oldest uniform I had. Some of the older members of the Squadron took up points of vantage around the ante-room, quietly supping ale and ready to give verbal encouragement to their respective sides.

Someone put his fingers to his mouth and blew a shrill note. The 'ball' was thrown in and battle commenced, accompanied by gasps, chokes, and adjectives. The scrum wheeled, straightened, and wheeled again, but the 'ball' remained locked in a cage of a dozen legs. I was in the middle as hooker, with Bill on my right and Star on my left, and I felt that we had a sound front; we would get that cushion out to the wing-men and score a try behind the piano.

Then someone slipped; the scrum became a heaving mass of humanity, legs, arms, and heads stuck out like an untidy cemetery, but the 'ball' was still covered. I wriggled my way out just in time to see our heftiest sergeant put his hands into the depths of the mound and withdraw a crumpled mass of feathers, twine, and cloth to which clung several arms. The owners of the arms had their eyes closed and their teeth were set like the proverbial bulldog's.

With one wrench the sergeant tore the 'ball' free and ran towards the swing-doors at our end of the room. I dived at his legs and he came down on the carpet, raising a cloud of dust. He wriggled free, but two opponents grabbed him from either side and tried to pull him down. Undaunted, the sergeant took them in his stride and lunged across the brass strip in the doorway, a fine try which was greeted with terrific cheering.

We sat down and had another round of drinks; few could stand, they were all exhausted. After a while a few challenges were flung out to all-comers to meet in mortal struggle as per the rules of all-in wrestling. Bill was the chief challenger, and he was soon matched by Percy. Someone volunteered to be manager, but before terms could be arranged the bout began. Advice was flung from all sides of the room as Bill and Percy, with their heads tucked under each other's shoulders, grimly strove for a throw. They eventually fell down together, and the result of the bout became a question of who could unravel himself first from the tangle of legs, arms, and torsos. By sheer weight Bill managed to get on top, claimed the fight and rolled off exhausted. The referees – the room was full of them – decided that it was a draw.

A final drink and the party broke up, all agreeing that sleep was essential before the big move south, and we bade good-night to our guests, who seemed to have had an enjoyable celebration; we certainly had.

Next morning came, August 29th. I had left a note for my batman to call me early and to pack a few things for me. He knew what was in the wind and whistled round my room with an air of the deepest satisfaction; he was an excellent chap.

I found most of the Squadron at the breakfast table; they were in a hurry and left one by one until only Star and I were left. We discussed a few final details and sorted out the pilots and aircraft. Bruno was on leave and it was arranged that he should collect an aircraft under repair at another aerodrome. The rest of the aircraft were serviceable, all on the top line, and we split them into two formations; I was to take the first lot and Star the second lot, after he had cleared everything up and thanked the Station C.O.

The weather was good; engines had been run up and details were known. I checked my maps, found everything ready, and told the crews to start up.

We took off, joined up and dived across the aerodrome, setting course for the south. We were to refuel at an aerodrome in Lincolnshire and then push on as fast as we could to relieve a Squadron coming north for a rest. When we landed there to refuel we found some pilots of this Squadron also refuelling. They had a lot to tell us, and their experiences did much to make our chaps all the more keen to get down into the battle zone.

We refuelled and took off, once more heading south and hoping we might run into something on the way. For that reason we flew stepped up and fairly well spaced out, the outer aircraft occasionally weaving to keep watch. The trip, however, was uneventful and we landed at our destination a few miles south of London. The Station C.O. greeted us and told us our allotted dispersal points. He gave us some idea of how things stood and we found him extremely helpful. Aircraft were dispersed and we had lunch.

I met several old friends in the mess and gleaned many useful pieces of information from them, especially concerning Hun tactics. One pilot whom I was very glad to see again had served in an Auxiliary Squadron for many years: I was looking forward to having a chat with him over a can of beer on some free night, but he was killed just after our arrival. I had been adjutant to his old Squadron for a time and knew him well; it was sad to see him go. I also met an old pupil there from Flying Training School days; he was doing well, had baled out three times and still came up for more; an astounding fellow! Another pilot I knew had served with me in Northern Ireland; he was also doing great things.

After lunch the pilots visited Station Operations and were given the roster for standing-to in readiness. We were told what to expect in the nature of surprise attacks, and consequently the number of pilots required to be within easy reach.

The rest of the Squadron arrived as we came from Operations, and I took over arrangements whilst Star went to make his number with the Station C.O. Their aircraft had hardly been dispersed when the transport aircraft arrived, bringing the crews and essential personnel, together with their tool-kits and light equipment. Things had been well organised, and in a very short space of time we were able to dispense with the generous help of the other Squadron on the aerodrome. Full of enthusiasm we volunteered to stand by with a Flight, and our offer was accepted, so we made up two Sections and stood by.

I HAD A ROW WITH A GERMAN

I still had my old machine, Star having taken over a new one and transferred his flag thereto. I had a big place in my heart for 'X' – that was her Squadron letter – and as I sat on a chock, eyeing her with well-deserved affection, I wondered what fortune would be hers, especially those eight Brownings tucked under her feathers.

Suddenly the loudspeakers broke the silence of the summer's afternoon. The other Squadron – they had Spitfires – had been ordered off. I watched them start up, taxi into wind and take off in quick succession, joining up as they climbed. Shortly afterwards we were ordered to be on our toes: 'Stand by'. I jumped into my aircraft, did up the harness, and plugged in 'phone lead and oxygen tube; the others did likewise. The crews were standing by the wing-tips of each aircraft and the starter batteries were connected up for instant starting.

We had not long to wait. I saw my fitter raise his thumb; the loudspeaker had spoken and we were to take off. I switched on, pressed the starter, and the Merlin roared into life. A runner came up to tell me to "Patrol base at 2,000 ft. and await orders."

We took off, all of the same mind, and cruised around at 2,000 ft. hoping for that elusive chance to get to grips with Fritz, but no further orders came over the radio telephone until the final order to land. There had been some activity to the east of us, but this had fizzled out and peace reigned again.

The rest of the day was uneventful, and towards dusk Star and I decided to do a little night flying to check up on local conditions. We took off as light failed and joined up, Star formating on my right. We flew around for about forty minutes, calling up Station Operations occasionally to test the radio telephone. It was good, and so were the Operations people; they knew their stuff and it gave us a lot of confidence. One had to have faith in the people on the ground, otherwise it was fatal in a jam. We landed and repaired to the mess. The anteroom was put out of action owing to a 'Jerry' bomb, and the occupants of the mess had congregated in the billiard-room: we joined them.

THE BLACK CROSS

Next morning, August 30th, I was up early, determined not to miss anything. Star had asked me the previous night to take turns leading the Squadron so that he could keep up with the paper-work. This suited me from the ground upwards and I felt buoyed up with new hopes. I had breakfast and wandered down to dispersal point. The Squadron was all set for anything with Star in command.

About 10 a.m., or it may have been later, they were ordered off. I stood by with the Emergency Section, but we were not required. The Squadron returned after about forty-five minutes, and we ran out to meet them, eager for results. Percy had shot down a Heinkel 111 near a neighbouring aerodrome: he got it at 2,000 ft.! Must have been a Nazi fanatic.

There were several more claims and Henry, the Squadron Intelligence Officer, started to sift the evidence. Jenks was missing, and we heard soon afterwards that he had tried to bale out but something had gone wrong: his blood-stained parachute arrived later and it was obvious that no attempt had been made to pull the rip-cord; he must have hit something getting out. Jenks was one of our best pilots and his death was a bitter blow for the Squadron.

I stood by for Star until shortly before lunch. His engine had been hit by an armour-piercing bullet and he spent some of the time checking up on the damage. One or two other aircraft had also been damaged and he was anxious to know the total effect on the state of serviceability.

Stand-off for lunch was arranged and I pushed off; but not for long. The Squadron was suddenly ordered off and I rushed back to take over the Emergency Section. I had been unlucky so far; this was the second Squadron show I had missed.

Bruno, Dopey, and I made up the Emergency Section and we climbed into our aircraft ready for take-off. We had only a few minutes to wait: I saw my fitter turn his head towards the tarmac and then jump up on to my port plane, stick his head into the cockpit and repeat the orders he had heard coming over the loudspeaker. We were to "Patrol base at 2,000 ft."

I HAD A ROW WITH A GERMAN

I took off, closely followed by Bruno on my right and Dopey on my left. At 1700 ft. Operations asked my height. I passed it back and received orders to climb to 20,000 ft. as fast as I could; they gave me a vector south-eastwards.

It was a perfect summer's day, the sky was cloudless, and as we approached 15,000 ft. the sun became dazzling, almost painful to the eyes. Somewhere below us the rest of the Squadron was mixed up in a scrap with Hun bombers attempting to attack our aerodromes, and I concluded that we were to keep some of their escort above them occupied.

To the north lay the sprawling mass of London and her suburbs, and the Thames could be seen winding its way through the maze of red, white, and black buildings on the waterfront towards the Estuary. Stretching from the south bank of the river towards the east and south, as far as the eye could see, lay the hazy outline of the Kentish coast; beneath were the rolling downs of wood and grassland, the heart of the county. I estimated our position to be three or four miles west of Maidstone, at a height of 17,000 ft., our course still south-easterly, when I heard Operations warning us of Hun aircraft in the vicinity. I intensified my search and rocked my aircraft to bring Bruno and Dopey further in; they were searching the flanks and keeping an eye on the area behind.

I had just steadied up and checked course when ahead and about 500 ft. above us I saw black crosses. There, shown up clearly by the sun, were rows and rows of Me.109s flying in 'Grid' formation, each row flying line astern slightly stepped up. They were travelling south-south-east, and I reckoned there were forty or fifty of them, perhaps more. There was no time to climb as we were already within range, and I knew they could out climb us if they wanted to. We had the advantage of the sun, however, being to starboard of them, and we drove straight into their flank to cut them up.

It was a sight worth all the months of waiting and disappointment.

All these particular Hun fighters were coloured silver against which the Black Cross stood out plainly, fitting emblem of what they represented. The nose, under-cowling, wing-tips, and tailplane tips were yellow, so was the under surface of the fuselage, hence the nickname of 'Yellow Bellies' by which they were known.

I had already turned the button to 'fire' and adjusted the reflector sight for '109s' now for some real practice. Taking a bead on the nearest aircraft – I was flying at about 20° to his line of flight and slightly below at about 175 yards distance – I pressed the button and saw the lines of incendiaries pouring out of the wings of my aircraft. The smell of cordite filled the cockpit and I felt the nose dip under the recoil; I held her steady. The Hun aircraft flew straight for a bit, then gently turned on its back. My shot appeared to be going straight into the engine cowling and cockpit, but as the Hun turned over, I saw what appeared to be tracers spiralling the fuselage and coming aft. I learnt months later from a fellow patient in hospital that this was shattered Perspex, the transparent material of which the cockpit cover was made; I must have been dumb not to realise that! The Hun turned slightly on his back and then dived beneath out of sight, going straight down; I had fired for about four seconds.

A shower of tracers whistled over my head and an orange-coloured streak, about an inch thick with a head the size of a tangerine, shrieked past the right side of my cockpit cover. I glanced in the mirror and saw a Hun about 200 yards aft; I dipped, turning slightly to the right, then pulled up again in a sharp left-hand turn. I could see nothing of Bruno or Dopey.

As I came up another Hun crossed my sights, he must have been about 120 yards off and flying steady. I gave him a burst and turned with him. A column of black smoke poured from what appeared to be the leading edge of his starboard wing, about a yard out from the wing-root; I thought my shot had gone slap into the fuselage. He turned across my path and his nose dropped into a dive, leaving a long column of smoke in his wake. I lost sight of him, having pulled up to avoid hitting him.

It was at this point that I nearly collided with another Hun. He flew past me only a few yards out and had obviously not seen me. He flew slightly across my sights, and at about 60 to 70 yards I gave him the works. It was too good to be true, few chances like this come one's way. I gave him a five-second burst in all; after three seconds of fire, he pulled the nose up, appeared to lose speed rapidly and then fell out of the sky, stalling into a dive; I gave him a bit more for luck. The cockpit seemed empty as he pulled up, but I saw no body come hurtling out.

I seemed now to be in the centre of the mass of Huns; they were all over the place but still trying to keep some semblance of formation. Tracers passed overhead and underneath, curving down ahead. I looked for another target, and as I turned to fly out towards the sun a Hun passed just to the right of me and slightly above. I raised the nose and turned, giving him all I had; I saw him roll on to his back, fly for a second inverted, then go straight down full out. My shot appeared to have gone into the lower half of the fuselage and belly, and I think I got the pilot as the armour plating does not protrude downwards as it does upwards in relation to the pilot's seat.

I was now out of ammunition and my mirror told me that three Huns, in line astern, were fastened on my tail. There was no sign of Bruno or Dopey, so I stuck the nose down, skidding and turning until I was diving all out. Glancing over my shoulder as I dived, I saw six Ju.87s in two lots of threes just to the east of me. They were going south in a great hurry and I bitterly regretted having to leave them alone. I pulled out gently at the bottom of the dive, turning to search above and behind, but I was not being followed. It was good to be in a Hurricane, especially in a jam; the Me.109s couldn't cope with them when it came to turning; they could dive and climb quicker than us but were not nearly so manoeuvrable.

I could still find no trace of Bruno and Dopey, so I returned to the aerodrome, landed, and taxied in. The Squadron was already down, and Henry was busy collating reports; they had had a good scrap and there were several claims, certainties and probables. I checked up on pilots and aircraft and found that Bruno and Dopey had not returned; I began to get worried, more so as time passed. News came through later that Bruno had force-landed and hurt his shoulder, but was otherwise O.K. I felt relieved; we could not afford to lose pilots, much less those of his experience. Dopey, however, was still missing. Days later, when in hospital, I heard he had been found; he had crashed and received fatal injuries. What toll he took of the enemy will never be known; the amount of lead flying about in that scrap could hardly have been for my sole benefit, and I know Bruno was out of the scrap right at the start. I like to think that Dopey got one, perhaps more; he was the youngest in the Squadron and a likeable chap.

Henry met me on the tarmac and asked for details. I gave him a brief account of the scrap and told him that I thought I had accounted for four Me.109s. He stated that unless I had seen them break up, catch fire, or crash, they could not be counted as destroyed. I could not state that, although I somehow felt that those Huns would not need rations any more. The Station Intelligence Officer gave me two probables and two possibles; he gave nothing away, and rightly so. That is why, when I read the official account of the Battle of Britain, I know in my own mind that those figures are the utter minimum; one could add another 1,000 Huns probably destroyed and still be within bounds. I can't imagine the German Luftwaffe having that faith.

I had late lunch and then stood by for Star. During the afternoon the other Squadron was sent off and we were told to be on our toes. The Huns were coming in from the south, and shortly afterwards Ack-Ack fire could be seen to the east of us. Then an air battle developed, and away up in the blue the glistening shapes of friend and foe could be seen twisting and turning to the accompaniment of machine-gun and cannon fire. Tracer streaks and vapour trails wove fantastic patterns against the blue sky, and the shrieks and whines of diving aircraft added sound to a scene hitherto undreamt of, even by writers of 'Air Ace' fiction. It was a grand sight, tragic no doubt, but nevertheless a scene more spectacular and stirring than any film studio could produce.

We saw the scrap fade out and the other Squadron return, refuel and rearm ready for further business. All was quiet until, just as we were arranging for tea, an order came through for us to stand by. We had two Sections ready. I had three aircraft in one and Bill had four in the other, and we climbed into our aircraft to await the signal to be off. The other Squadron was already on its way to attack another raid coming north and we were hoping to be sent up to deal with any Hun escort or following raids.

Instructions came through to take off more quickly than we had dared to hope: "Patrol base at 1,500 ft." We were off and climbing fast in a few seconds, and I could see Bill way out on my right coming up like a shell; the rest were strung out behind racing for position. I turned left for a wide circuit, easing up a bit, and my No.2 and No.3 closed in. Then I heard Operations calling again: "Climb to 15,000 ft. as fast as you can go," came the controller's voice, shortly followed by instructions to proceed on a certain vector. Bill had heard it too, and I saw him, through the mirror, closing in astern and stepping up.

I set course for the south, and when we had reached a point a few miles south-east of Tunbridge Wells, at a height of about 14,000 ft., Bill informed me that he had seen something to the east of us. He had already turned his Section, and I opened up the throttle to regain position. The aircraft we were chasing proved to be Hurricanes on another scent, and Bill turned, rocking his wings as a signal. He was now slightly above and ahead of my Section, and I manoeuvred to get the lead again.

We were flying south with the sun on our right, climbing once more, and keeping an eye on the sun side as the Hun had the advantage in that respect most of the day when coming in, an advantage which they never failed to use. At 17,000 ft. I had drawn almost level with Bill's Section when I heard the rat-tat of machine-gun fire, punctuated by the chug-chug of cannons, and tracer streaks and cannon-shell tracks appeared over his Section as several Me.109s came hurtling down on their tails.

There were about seven in one batch, followed by six more; the odds were two to one, which was more than even: some people reckoned three to one was evens by this time. I turned, and we waded into them. The fight became a wheeling mixture of Me.109s and Hurricanes; each one seemed to be firing at the chap in front of him. Two aircraft, one a few feet above the other, were both firing at something in front; a horrible sight for a Life Insurance Company to see. I was about to pick out a possible victim for burial when I saw a Me.109 fastened on to the tail of a Hurricane, blowing bits of fabric and wood off the fuselage with machine-gun and cannon fire.

My blood boiled; no darned Hun would get away with that. I opened the throttle wide and raced after him, opening fire at something like 180 to 200 yards, all three of us, with the Me.109 in the middle, being in line astern and turning slightly. I gained on the Hun rapidly; he had obviously slowed down to keep on the Hurricane's tail and appeared not to notice me. I kept the button pressed the whole time, determined to get him before he finished off the Hurricane. My firing sight packed up as I closed in, but as I was now only about 70 yards astern of the Hun, I was able to use the tracks of the incendiaries as a sighting. My shot appeared to be going home, yet he still maintained formation although I could not see if he was firing or not, due to the firework display from my own guns.

Then gradually he rolled to the right on to his back and flew inverted for a while. I kept on firing. I was almost on top of him now, and saw patches of black material coming away from the starboard wing near the wing-root and from the fuselage. A piece of long wire or metal dropped off as the Hun turned, still inverted, and then gradually dropped away into a dive, turning slowly. I wanted to follow him down and see him crash, but a glance in the mirror made me change my mind. There were three Huns on my tail, the nearest only about

I HAD A ROW WITH A GERMAN

100 yards astern. Why he never opened fire I do not know. I can only assume that he was afraid of hitting his compatriot in front of me.

I had now only a few rounds left in the guns, less than ten apiece, and once again I relied on the good offices of the Hurricane to get me out of a jam. I flicked over to the left and pulled the stick back hard, diving, turning, and skidding down to 10,000 ft., but by then the Hun had disappeared. What speed I reached in that dive I do not know; the needle had passed maximum figure long before I levelled out, but it certainly added even further to my confidence in the strength of the Hurricane. I eased the nose up, climbing like a rocket with all that stored-up speed; it was one of the finest thrills I have ever experienced in my years of flying.

I turned south again in the hope of picking up some of the Squadron, but when I reached the scene – it was on the coast near Dungeness – everyone had vanished. It has always been a thing of wonder to me how an area full of whirling aircraft can suddenly become completely vacant; I could not have been away more than a minute and not a trace of anything remained. I returned to the aerodrome, wondering how many were safe, where that battered Hurricane had gone down, and who was flying it: had he got away with it? I somehow felt he could not have made his base after that beating-up. I was wrong!

I landed, taxied in, and there on the tarmac was the very machine. I had been unable to read the Squadron letter in the scrap, but the damage was identical. How the pilot ever managed to fly home I do not know. Flaps, undercarriage, elevators, and rudder, which now consisted of a few tubes and thin air, still worked; they must have done. No recommendation for British aircraft construction could ever surpass that amazing example of sheer aeronautical guts.

Clustered around the battered but unbent aircraft were people from all parts of the Station. I joined the spectators and asked who had been flying it; it was 'The Colonel'. I saw him talking to Bill in the middle of an inquisitive crowd of pilots. He was giving vent to his feelings and his opinion of the Huns in general, particularly the one who had written his name on the poor old Hurricane. 'The Colonel' had a very good command of the English language, both written and unwritten – though muttered in secret places – but no oration, however eloquent, could have matched this piece of verbal cannon-fire. Roars of laughter assured him of full agreement all round, and he seemed better for the outburst.

I gave Henry a verbal account of the scrap and heard a few minutes later that my Me.109 was confirmed, although I never knew whether it crashed on land or in the sea. I had the satisfaction, however, of knowing that at least one Hun had been added to the Squadron's collection. This stood at something like 12 confirmed and 12 probables from the Dunkirk show, and now, the first day with the Huns in the Blitz, I estimated that we had shot down 14 altogether. When the final figures arrived from Operations, we were given something like 7 confirmed and 5 or 6 probables, a very gratifying day. Star was very bucked, and I was feeling like someone in another world: I had kept my vow.

One incident, however, spoilt my sense of accomplishment. News came through that Dicky, one of our sergeants who, unknown to me, had been missing, had been riddled by a Hun whilst coming down by parachute. It may be permissible in war to shoot someone descending by parachute from a wrecked or burning aircraft, though he is using the direct and indisputable counterpart of a lifeboat, but only those devoid of all sense of fair fight and chivalry could do it. Paratroops are different; they drop under special conditions and are 'offensive troops' in no less a degree than a landing party by boat. I felt bitter about Dicky and so did Star, but little did he know that next day he was to meet the same fate.

We were off that evening, and spent most of the time in the billiard-room comparing notes. One thing always stands out clearly in my mind when I recall those times. Contrary to what one would suppose, there is no sense of strain or tension in a scrap, nor for some time afterwards. It is when one settles down to lounge, smoke, and

I HAD A ROW WITH A GERMAN

perhaps enjoy a can of beer that fatigue becomes apparent: a feeling of pleasant drowsiness from which one has no wish to be disturbed. This was how I felt at any rate, and I found a great deal of will power necessary to rouse myself somewhere about ten o'clock and push off to bed.

Next morning, August 31st, I was down at dispersal point before breakfast. It was another grand day, full of expectations: would the Hun oblige?

All was quiet, and I wandered back towards the mess. On the way I stopped and chatted to an anti-aircraft machine-gunner. He had a battery of Lewis guns ingeniously mounted on a home-made stand. He had had the same instrument in France and, thanks to its prolific output of hot lead and the accuracy of the gunner, several Huns had come to a sticky end. The gunner had a fine sense of humour, unimpaired by his experiences in the evacuation from France.

After breakfast I spent some time in the portable Squadron office whilst Star stood by. There was some activity during the morning and the Squadron was eventually sent off. We, that is the Emergency Section, stood by, but were not required. The Squadron returned in due course, several aircraft being damaged. They had had a scrap and shot up a Hun formation; the results were now being sifted. Star was missing, and I feared the worst: Jerry always paid particular attention to leaders of formations. I wandered over to the Station Aircraft Repair Section to check up on the number of aircraft I could raise to fill up depleted Sections.

The Station C.O. arrived shortly afterwards and informed me that Star had baled out but the Hun had shot him dead on the way down. I could hardly believe that this could be the end of Star. That a fellow of his ability and charm, a fellow who had the right idea about everything and only wished to do his job in complete accord with all, regardless of rank, should die like this was too much.

I went back to the dispersal point and broke the news to the Squadron. Nothing can describe their feelings; they were expressed by all, crews and pilots alike, in no uncertain terms. Tempers were raised to white heat; nothing that they had heard or read could ever have brought home to them more forcibly the ruthless type we were fighting against. Their determination to smash the Hun now knew no bounds. Although they had missed the first mass raids of the Blitz, their subsequent efforts bear testimony to the fact that this act profited the Hun nothing.

With the help of Bill, I arranged for two Sections to stand by, the remainder of the Squadron to push off to the mess for an early lunch. 'The Colonel' had taken over Bruno's Flight, and it was his turn to stand off: we remained on duty.

Relief had been arranged for lunch, and I had just started off for the mess when the order came through for all our available aircraft to take off. A large raid was coming in from the south, and the lull of the past two hours or so changed to frenzied activity.

I grabbed my helmet and parachute and ran to the aircraft which I was to use in place of 'X', which I had lent to another pilot during a previous raid when it had been damaged. The crew had already started up – they never needed asking – and I jumped in.

We received orders to join up with another Squadron at 2,000 ft. over the aerodrome, and in a few seconds were climbing up as hard as we could go. The Sections formed up as we climbed, and I turned slightly at 1,000 ft. to make a wide circuit and to look out for the other Squadron, which, a few seconds later, I saw coming south, flying in an inverted 'J' formation; one Flight was in 'Vic' with the other in line astern behind the left-hand man of the leading Flight. We followed suit, but joining up on the right, thus making a total formation in the shape of an inverted 'U'.

After a few minutes we turned north, and I glanced up to see what we were chasing. Right above us were rows of Hun bombers – Ju.88s in line astern – and my aircraft were directly below one line of them and closing distance rapidly. We were soon within about 1,000 ft. of them, well within cannon range and approaching machine-gun range,

I HAD A ROW WITH A GERMAN

but the formation was still going ahead. I did some rapid thinking; if we maintained our position we would, in a few seconds, be sitting shots for both front and rear Hun gunners. I therefore decided to attack before they had a chance to open fire, and certainly before we came within danger of collision. I rocked my wings and then eased the nose up, taking a bead on No.5 of the line of Huns and giving him a raking burst.

I turned on to my side as I finished firing, kicked hard on bottom rudder to fake a stalled turn, and dived down, straightening out as I gathered speed. I repeated the process on No.3 and, glancing over my shoulder as I skidded sideways over the top, saw clouds of greyish-white smoke issuing from his port engine. I could not see the effect of my fire on No.5, he was too far behind. I was about to pull up to attack No.1, who incidentally was now losing height preparatory to a dive-bomb attack, when I heard a metallic click above the roar of my engine. It seemed to come from the starboard wing and I glanced in that direction, but a sudden burst of heat struck my face, and I looked down into the cockpit.

A long spout of flame was issuing from the hollow starboard wing-root, curling up along the port side of the cockpit and then across towards my right shoulder. I had seen neither tracers nor cannon tracks near my aircraft; the fire could not have been caused by structural or other failure, and I therefore presumed I had picked up a stray incendiary. I had some crazy notion that if I rocked the aircraft and skidded, losing speed, the fire might go out. Not a bit of it; the flames increased until the cockpit was like the centre of a blow-lamp nozzle.

There was nothing left to do but bale out: a forced landing was out of the question as I was still 7,000 to 8,000 ft. up. I reached down to pull the radio telephone 'phone lead out of its socket, but the heat was too great. The skin was already rising off my right wrist and hand, and my left hand was starting to blister, the glove being already partially burnt off. My shoes and slacks must have been burning all this time, but I cannot remember any great pain.

Shock is nature's anaesthetic; a blessing I now know to the full; something that hides the pain and blanks the mind, leaving a memory of something unpleasant yet a feeling that one has defeated that which was once a terrifying thought. I think that is why I still yearn to fly again, am still willing to take the chance and risk, without which life would be a monotonous existence, unworthy to be called 'living'.

I undid my harness and tried to raise myself, but found I had not the strength. I was comforted by the thought that I had my gun ready loaded if things came to the worst. I decided to pull off my helmet, open the cockpit cover and roll on my back so that I could drop out. My helmet came off after a determined tug: I opened the cockpit cover and that was the last effort I had to make. There was a blinding flash, I seemed to be travelling through yards of flame; then I found myself turning over and over in the air, but with no sense of falling. Gradually I ceased to travel forwards and fell downwards, still turning head over heels. My hand instinctively passed over the harness release and on to the rip-cord handle. I pulled hard and felt the cord being drawn through the strongly woven fabric tubing; then came a gentle jerk as I was pulled into the vertical position, swinging comfortably, secure in my harness. An interminable space of time seemed to have elapsed whilst I was endeavouring to escape from that inferno, but actually it was less than a minute.

Everything was quiet, deathly still, an amazing contrast to the sound of flight. I remember thinking how grand the scene below me looked; fields of green grass, fields of stubble patched here and there with clumps of trees and hedgerows. Country lanes wound their way from farm to highway where the metallic surface seemed to shimmer in the heat. I had always longed to make a 'brolley jump', as a parachute descent is called in the Service, but now I could raise no enthusiasm as I floated down. Only the earth below had any interest for me; I was feeling distinctly 'browned off'.

As I approached the earth, I seemed to gather speed; the swinging appeared to be accentuated, and the sight of a barbed-wire fence below gave my fuzzled mind a start. I was then about 50 ft. up, and as I went through the last swinging motion the fence disappeared from view, the ground came up in an unfriendly way, and I closed my eyes. I felt my left hip and head strike the ground simultaneously and then all was still.

I sat up and looked around, and was surprised that I had not received any injury from my impact with the ground. Then I remembered the days of instruction in 'how to use a parachute'; how one should relax when striking the ground and on no account try to take weight on the feet. I never intended to take any weight on my feet, I was too 'disinterested'.

With an effort I stood up and surveyed the damage. My shoes still looked like shoes and I found I could walk; why, I don't know, as my ankle and each side of my right foot were burnt and my left foot was scorched and had several small burns. My slacks had disappeared except for portions that had been covered by the parachute harness. The skin on my right leg, from the top of the thigh to just above the ankle, had lifted and draped my leg like outsize plus-fours. My left leg was in a similar condition except that the left thigh was only scorched, thanks to the flames having been directed to my right side.

Above each ankle I had a bracelet of unburnt skin: my socks, which were always wrinkled, had refused to burn properly and must have just smouldered. That my slacks should have burnt so easily is not surprising; oil mist percolates one's clothing, and I probably had enough on my person to lubricate a battleship. My Service gloves were almost burnt off, and the skin from my wrists and hands hung down like paper bags. The underside of my right arm and elbow were burnt and so was my face and neck. I could see all right, although it felt like looking through slits in a mass of swollen skin, and I came to the conclusion that the services of a doctor were necessary.

There seemed to be nobody about, so I decided to walk to the end of the field where I could see a gate. I remember calling out in the hope that someone would come along as I made my way across the grass. I reached the gate, managed to open it, and found myself in a country lane. Lower down, on the opposite side of the lane, was a cowshed, and I walked towards it. A man came out; he had apparently heard me calling, and when he saw me, he stopped and stared. I guessed I must be looking a little strange, and promptly blurted out, "R.A.F. pilot. I want a doctor." Then I sat down on the green verge of the lane; I was feeling tired and more 'browned off' than ever.

That man proved a good Samaritan. He put me on his back and carried me a good quarter of a mile to the farmhouse higher up the lane. It was a hot day and uphill all the way, but he refused to put me down for a rest even when I asked him to.

We were met at the door of the house by the farmer's wife. She took one look at me, then darted into a room on the left of the doorway instructing my gallant bearer to follow suit. The room was as clean as a new pin, well furnished and well carpeted, and in the centre was a large bed made up with spotless linen sheets and pillow-slips.

"Lay him down there," she said. I protested vigorously, for I was oozing like a sponge; to place me on this beautiful bed seemed sacrilege, much as I longed to lie down and pass out. But the farmer's wife wouldn't take 'no' for an answer, and I was laid down and given a mixture of brandy and something else. It made me sit up for a bit, but did me good.

I remember asking repeatedly for a doctor – I was still feeling very 'browned off' – and I was told to take it easy, a car had been sent for. When I look back, I feel ashamed of myself for all the trouble I must have given her. No one could have done more for me than she did, and I shall always be grateful to her.

A car duly arrived; it belonged to the local air raid warden and he took charge of me. He was accompanied by an R.A.F. friend of his who happened to be on leave and who, incidentally, collected my parachute later and handed it over to a near-by R.A.F. Station. Between them they managed to get me into the car and, after making me as comfortable as possible on the back seat, we pushed off for a nearby war hospital.

For the first time since baling out – or rather being blown out – I became aware of physical pain as we sped along in the car. It was an open four-seater with hood and side screens, and the draught through the gaps between the screens played on my burns until I began to ask "How much further?", a question I repeated with increasing frequency. The warden-driver was going as fast as he could and I must have known it, but I kept on asking. I hope I meet that gentleman again one day to offer my apologies; he is another of those to whom I am deeply indebted.

After what seemed hours, we arrived at the war hospital; we had actually been about fifteen minutes getting there, a distance of five or six miles through winding country lanes. I was wheeled in and laid on a bed in a small room annexed to a large ward. Doctors and nurses arrived, my remaining clothes were cut off, and I was given an injection of something, probably morphia.

I lay there for a short while, my burns covered with damp gauze. Then the trolley arrived and I was wheeled into the operating theatre; a painless jot in my arm and I passed into oblivion.

From that moment I started to accumulate a debt that mounted daily, and still mounts; a debt I can never repay, against which human thanks seem utterly inadequate. Every time I see a nurse or a doctor now, I feel a hidden sense of humility, prompted not only by the ceaseless care and attention I received and still receive from them, but also by what I saw them do for others far worse than myself, all but dead casualties who have become living miracles.

Chapter 3

The Red Cross

Beams of coloured light crossed my eyes, moving downwards, distorted, unsteady, like the rays of light penetrating the moving waters of an aquarium. In the background a large square screen of white seemed to ripple, grow large then small again; to the sides a pale-green border tapered off to infinity, and across the whole fantastic pattern two beams of piercing light slashed their tracks. The sound of voices, of movement, filled my ears, undefinable yet real, fading, rising to a crescendo, then fading again. I tried to move but I seemed to have no strength, only my eyes and ears appeared to exist; not even the flicker of an eyelid replied to my efforts.

Then the scene before me changed; the moving, unsteady ribbons of coloured liquid light became still; they took on a new shape and turned to natural colour and shade. Sound became definable; voices became few, rational, and quiet, no longer fading but close to, and of even gentle tone.

I was lying on my back gazing at the white ceiling of my room. Beyond and to the sides I could see the green walls, and to the left were two windows through which poured the strong rays of the mid-morning sun. I turned my head slightly, that was all I could do, and bending over me I saw the face of my nurse. On her head she wore the dazzling snow-white headgear of her profession, traditional reminder of a noble woman, forerunner of countless Sisters of Mercy. Then the light failed and I slipped back into oblivion.

After what seemed an interminable age, I awoke. I was being lifted, higher, higher. Several nurses and patients, in hospital blue, were moving me, complete with mattress and bedding. I was no longer being lifted, now I was being lowered until I felt a slight jar; I was on the floor. They were pushing me under a meshwork of iron girders and wire springs; it was my bedstead. Then another mattress was placed above me, partially shutting out the light. I lay still. Suddenly the sound of something familiar, something that seemed to take me back to times long past, brought me to my senses. The chug-chug of cannon-fire, the rat-tat of machine-guns, and the whine and scream of diving and zooming aircraft broke the silence of my 'air raid shelter'.

"There's a battle going on overhead," said my nurse. She was sitting on the floor by my side.

Above the noise I heard the unmistakable scream of an engine turning at ever-increasing speed. The sound grew louder and louder until the very floor seemed to reverberate with the echo. Then suddenly it stopped, cut to silence, and I heard an excited voice somewhere outside shout, "There's one down." Gradually the noise died away, nurses and patients lifted me back on to the bed, and I fell asleep.

When I awoke, I found a new nurse in my room. She was the night nurse, busy opening the windows wide and drawing-to the black-out curtains. A reading-lamp provided a mellow light, soothing to burnt eyes, and I ventured to sum up my surroundings. I asked the nurse where I was, and she told me that I was in a room annexed to a large ward. The building was of wood, one of many built in the last war to form a war hospital, and now once again converted to its original role. "We have several R.A.F. pilots in here as well as many Dunkirk casualties, including some Frenchmen," she added.

I was now fully awake and not 'seeing things'; an easy thing to do when sleeping with one's eyes open! I felt hot and was becoming aware of a terrible thirst. My body seemed drained of moisture and I pleaded for a long cool drink.

"You can have all that you can drink," said the nurse; "in fact you must drink at least 120 oz. of liquid a day, whether you are thirsty or not."

THE RED CROSS

I needed no encouragement; I could have drained a large-sized pond there and then. A glass of cold fruit juice was put to my lips and I drank the precious liquid.

Somewhere in the distance I heard a siren wailing 'The Devil's Lament', and within a few minutes I was once again in my 'air raid shelter'. Then I heard the drone of the Hun up above. The floor shook as the A.A. guns opened up, and I could hear the whistle of bombs.

My nurse knelt down beside me, bending over my chest with one hand on my shoulder and the other resting on the cage over my legs. There was a terrific 'crump', then another and another. The building seemed to leave the ground and come back with a sickening thud again and again. Then there came a lull. I asked for a drink and some ice; it was stifling; my mouth was parched and the corners of it seemed to tear apart as I tried to speak. Nurse brought a bowl of ice cubes and a glass of iced water which I drank with relish. Then she placed some ice in my mouth, repeating the process every ten minutes or so; it was delicious.

Again, we heard the drone of the Hun, and then the bombs came crashing down around us. It went on for hours, and all the time my nurse crouched down beside me, placing more ice in my mouth and adjusting my pillow from time to time to make me more comfortable. She gave me some tablets; these were to make me sleep, and they did, for in a few moments I had passed out.

One afternoon, it may have been next day, I was awake. Sister came in and said my wife had arrived. I was well enough to worry about her seeing me as I was: my hands, forearms, and legs were encased in dried tannic acid; my face, which felt the size of the proverbial melon, was treated in the same way, and I peered through slits in the mask. I heard footsteps approaching the bed, and then saw my wife standing gazing at me. She flushed a little and said, "What on earth have you been doing with yourself, darling?"

I found it hard to answer.

"Had a row with a German," I replied.

She tried to smile, and sat down by my side. She told me that the Superintendent of the hospital had sent her a telegram saying I was dangerously ill, so she had left straight away, and after a difficult journey had managed to find the hospital. She was going back for our son in a few days to take him to her people on the South Coast, where she could look after him and be much nearer to me. The local hotels were full, but some kind-hearted people had found her temporary lodgings where she could come and go as she pleased.

Then it was time for her to go; I hated her leaving.

"I'll be back first thing in the morning," she promised. I remembered her going, then nothing more.

The next few weeks are a confused tangle of events all out of place, yet I can recall several incidents quite plainly.

My burns had turned septic, and from then on, I lived in a world half real, half fanciful. I can recall seeing my wife at intervals; my batman and the flight-sergeant came several times; a Group Captain commanding a near-by Fighter Station called in; Bruno had tea with me, he was just out of hospital. I remember telling Bruno that I would be out in three or four weeks on the job again; he must have smiled to himself. Interspersed with these events I had crazy deliriums, most of them humorous.

One night I was in my 'air raid shelter', but in my flight of fancy it had changed to a lounge, the ceiling of which was extremely low, in fact people were walking about ducking their heads. I became involved in a heated argument, about what I do not know. Somebody insulted somebody else and, filled with righteous indignation, I tried to get up to settle the miscreant. People were trying to hold me down, but I lashed out right and left, sometimes burying my hands in the ceiling and bringing plaster down on the floor. Then I came-to. The night nurse seemed exhausted and the bed-clothes and cage were awry. I felt sorry for the nurse; the Hun had been bombing all that night, and that was enough to put up with without the 'troubles' of an unruly patient.

THE RED CROSS

Another night, for some inexplicable reason, I thought I had been detailed to interview female applicants for very secret jobs in the Operations room at Fighter Headquarters. I was at a Station in Northern Ireland, why I do not know, and seated before me was an applicant for this work. I asked her where she was employed.

"All over the place," she replied.

I became suspicious. "Where do you live?" I asked.

"Oh, anywhere," she answered.

This was too much; I must check up on her. I asked her to pass the 'phone to me, it was on the shelf. She said it wouldn't work. There was a cupboard on my left, and on the top of it my clerk was stretched out fast asleep. I thought it would be a pity to wake him as he was probably tired, so I asked the applicant to go to the guard-room and bring the guard along. She refused, and what was more she laughed, and kept on laughing.

I was furious and was just about to give her a piece of my mind when I awoke. The night nurse was still laughing, and had been the 'applicant'. The 'telephone on the shelf' turned out to be a bottle of medicine, and the 'sleeping clerk' a blanket tucked in along the rail holding up the black-out curtains. Days passed; how many I do not know; then gradually things seemed to take a more orderly course. I began to appreciate time, to enjoy the radio programmes and view the day's happenings in better perspective. I may have occasionally 'ordered the Squadron off', in fact I have a shrewd suspicion that I told my wife to 'get off the ground as fast as she could' several times, but these fanciful flights became less and less frequent.

Then my insides 'packed up', due to my toxic condition. I felt like a tube-station through which much traffic passed ceaselessly, and back I went again to the land of delirious imagination. The surgeon visited me more frequently; he was a great fellow – a New Zealander – with a reputation for lawn tennis as well as surgery. Sister kept popping in, sometimes accompanied by the anaesthetist or the house surgeon; I remember them vaguely in my wanderings.

I HAD A ROW WITH A GERMAN

For several days I imagined I lived on a farm. I was ill and blamed the drainage system; the ditches were badly kept; the sluice was choked; I raised Cain. I invited hundreds of experts down to advise me on the matter. It was no good, I still felt ill. Then I had a brainwave and called in the local Water Board – it must be the water. They were indignant, so was I; I raised more Cain. Eventually I ceased to worry about my farm. One evening I was sitting on a fence surveying the stock and pastureland; I attempted to climb down – and then suddenly found reason again. My nurse was gently pushing me back into the hollow of the bed. From then on, I rapidly became normal, began to feel better, and altogether made slow but steady progress.

As I improved so I became more sensitive to pain. Everything that could be done for me was done, but I began to dread the dawn. One day Sister came in and said, "Somebody has been on the 'phone asking if you would like to be transferred to an R.A.F. hospital up North."

I said, "No, I want to stay here," and so I remained. I could not bring myself to leave those who had been so good to me; nothing was ever too much for them, and it was due to their tireless efforts that I still existed.

As I improved, I received more visitors, including the hospital barber. A local padre called occasionally, and we chatted about the war and other things; some of the R.A.F. pilots came also, and talked shop. I was now eating well and sleeping without persuasion; in fact, I began to live again.

Sometimes I was wheeled out into the sun on a spinal carriage. My eyes were covered with some blue transparent material, but it was good to be out once more and to feel the cool breeze playing on my hands and face. More than once I was rushed back to cover when a scrap developed overhead.

Then one evening I was asked if I would like to visit the Officers' Ward; there was a birthday party in progress and they would like me to go. I enjoyed that party, and a few days later was moved into the

THE RED CROSS

ward; I was now fit to be at large. Blossom, my day nurse, came with me, and I found the company of other patients a great comfort.

I had hardly settled down there when an R.A.F. consulting surgeon came to see me, and shortly after he had gone Sister informed me that I was to be transferred; I was to go next day; everything was being arranged. My new hospital specialised in skin grafting and plastic surgery, and had also a new treatment for burns which would do my leg good.

Next morning 'Scotty', the staff nurse, packed my things. The ambulance arrived, and I bade goodbye to 'Fluid', my next-door neighbour, and the other patients. Sister and Blossom came to see me off. The driver of the ambulance, a member of the A.T.S., started up, a last shout of farewell, the doors closed and we were off. I was leaving friends to whom I was indebted beyond human measure.

I had company in the ambulance, an orderly and another patient; the latter was 'mobile', going to the same hospital. I asked them where we were heading. "South," said the orderly, "about fifteen or twenty miles, on the Kent-Sussex border."

He lit a cigarette for me and asked if I was comfortable. I had not been able to take the cage with me as it would not fit in, and the weight of the clothes pressed on my burns.

"Could you stop every fifteen minutes or so?" I asked.

"Certainly," he replied, and straightway tapped on the window of the driver's cabin. We pulled up, my blankets were rearranged, and some chocolate was produced and handed round. This process was repeated several times until we eventually reached the new hospital.

I was wheeled along covered walks into a large wooden building, a general ward. The A.T.S. driver patted my hands, now free of tannic, wished me luck and was away – the end of a brief but pleasant acquaintance.

I was soon settled in bed, and an R.A.F. corporal came up to my side and chatted with me. He was in charge of the R.A.F. orderlies who worked the special salt bath for burns, a new treatment I was to enjoy to the full. He had spent many years in the Service, finishing his time and then rejoining on the outbreak of war, and he assured me that in this hospital they could do almost anything for anybody. He was obviously taking stock of my face and I thought he was merely being comforting, but when I think of the amazing recoveries I have since witnessed those words of his now seem very mild.

Lunch was served to me, and afterwards the Sister came to my bedside and asked for many particulars. She told me that I could have my first salt bath that evening, and I began to wonder how it would affect me; if it would sting; if the dressings would come away without the painful coaxing and tugging necessary under ordinary conditions.

Bath-time arrived and the corporal, together with two orderlies, wheeled my bed into the canvas-walled 'Spa'. A canopy supported by four long steel pillars covered the bed, and attached to the frame of the canopy were powerful heating lamps. On the left of the bed-space was the bath, a large porcelain affair, and on the far wall a maze of water-pipes and gadgets were fixed.

As I was being prepared for the treatment the corporal enlightened me on the functioning of the apparatus. The bath was filled with a solution of hot water and salt, and a complicated system of supply pipes and syphons drew off one gallon per minute from the bath, replacing it with an equal amount of fresh salt water of the same strength and at a set temperature. A large gauge above the control board indicated the setting, and should the temperature rise above a certain limit – which might prove uncomfortable for the patient – warning of this would be given by an electric buzzer.

I was lowered into the bath, complete with dressings. I had already told the Sister that the gauze on my right shin had been on for two or three days; it had refused to come off despite much effort.

"Let the dressings soak for a while," she said as she came in; "they will soon come off and then we can see the extent of the burns."

Contrary to my expectation, I found the bath very pleasant, and after about fifteen minutes I ventured to move my legs. My right leg was half-bent and solid and I had no movement in the knee, but I managed to move the whole limb from the hip. I saw gauze floating on the surface and gradually the red outline of my leg came into view. My dressings had floated off; I nearly passed out with relief.

My facial burns were examined first. The neck, cheeks, nose, and lower forehead had healed, although they had contracted somewhat due to the tannic acid.

My eyelids needed treatment. My left wrist, right forearm, and elbow were covered with new skin, but my right wrist was still uncovered. My hands had healed, and luckily only one finger suffered from contraction. A narrow strip on the left shin remained open but was considered a minor affair. The right leg was the chief item of interest and this received particular attention. An oblong area on the inside of the leg, about four inches wide and stretching from just above the ankle to the top of the thigh, required covering.

The investigation over, I was lifted from the bath and thoroughly dried under the heating lamps. My burns were covered with 'Tulle Gras', a network of large mesh dipped in vaseline and some antiseptic solution which prevented the gauze, when laid on the top, from adhering to the flesh – a marvellous invention.

I was soon back in the ward, feeling very refreshed. That night I made the acquaintance of 'Mother', the night nurse. She came along with the dressing trolley to moisten the gauze on my legs and wrist with warm saline, as it was essential that these dressings be kept damp. I slept like a top that night.

Days passed. My wife came to see me; she had found lodgings nearby and had arranged to come every week for a day and a night.

I was soon able to sit up, survey the ward and meet my fellow patients, and with the passing of time I rapidly gathered strength. I now knew no pain, only a yearning to be up and about; to be with my family; to fly again in that world above earthly things where I had known so much joy.

I HAD A ROW WITH A GERMAN

My fellow patients were from various Services and walks of life. To the left of me were Perky, an R.A.F. pilot, and Poley Boy, a Polish Squadron Leader. The latter had just been decorated by General Sikorski, the Polish Commander-in-Chief, and congratulations were still being showered upon him by members of the staff. To my right was Josef, a Czecho-Slovakian sergeant pilot. Opposite were Jack, a New Zealander, Neville, and a sergeant, all R.A.F. pilots. We were all burnt to approximately the same extent and in the same places, and thus were of a kind.

Further along the ward were Buster, an air-gunner with a lacerated leg resulting from a crash in a war-damaged aircraft; Joe, another air-gunner, who came off a motor-cycle whilst in motion; Noisy, an Army casualty from Dunkirk who had lost his voice; Sidi Barrani of the Pioneer Corps, another road casualty; Yorky, a Dunkirk casualty who had lost most of his face and was now receiving a new one (his hands were fingerless and badly burnt, little could be done for them); Reggie, an R.A.F. bomber pilot with a badly burnt hand received in a crash after a long raid over Germany; Jonah, an A.F.S. casualty from London, also with badly burnt hands; Radio, an A.R.P. worker who had been discharged from the Army after being seriously wounded in France and who had now lost an eye in the Battle of 'Goering *v.* John Citizen'; George, a member of a Bomb Disposal Squad who had lost both eyes and had received several shrapnel wounds when disposing of a bomb which, unfortunately, exploded during the process. He was the sole survivor of a party of twelve, and to my mind there is no medal, nor words big enough, to equal the measure of courage and bravery that he displayed. There were other patients too whom I cannot recall but who, like those I have mentioned, were to prove most worthy company.

One day 'The Maestro' toured the ward, and I met him for the first time. He was accompanied by Doc, the house surgeon, and they came over to my bedside to weigh up the work to be done on my face. The first facial grafts I needed were eyelids, top and bottom. My burns were healing rapidly, I could see new skin each time I visited the 'Spa', but 'The Maestro' intended to speed the process still further.

"We will pinch-graft the two large patches on your leg and give you new top eyelids first," he said. "Your eyes will be covered for a week, but it's worth it."

The day dawned for the 'op'. Inwardly apprehensive and outwardly unconcerned, I was given an injection which quickly produced a parched mouth followed by a thirst that can only be estimated in gallons. Shortly afterwards I was wheeled into the annexe to the theatre, given another injection, and knew no more.

When I awoke I was in darkness. I felt good though weak, and heard the nurse asking if I would like a drink. I was feeling hungry as well as thirsty, and asked for some bread and butter and tea, which duly arrived, and I was fed piece-meal.

I was blindfolded for nearly seven days and, although time dragged on slowly, the care of Sister and the nurses, combined with the unselfish attention of my fellow patients, made life much more pleasant than I had dared to hope. Every hour throughout the day, one or other of the 'mobile' patients would light a cigarette for me, place it between my lips, and chat to me until it was finished. Those smokes became something to look forward to, a delightful break in the monotony of my existence; I could have been among few better friends.

Then, at last, the bandages were removed from my eyes. The light hurt at first, but gradually I became accustomed to sight once more, and in half an hour or so I was gazing in a mirror admiring my new eyelids. They came from under my left arm above the elbow, but I felt no pain from that source – in fact it had healed when the dressing was removed later.

Then my leg was uncovered and I saw a pinch-graft for the first time. 'Doc' was pleased with the result; this had been his part of the 'op'.

In sixteen days those two large patches were covered with skin; incredible but true. I had watched a film spread over the flesh between the grafts, which themselves appeared not to change.

I received new bottom eyelids shortly afterwards, and was soon able to do everything but walk. All my burns were healed and I could use my hands almost normally. One evening I was lifted into an invalid chair, and I propelled myself around the ward returning many calls and exchanging experiences.

Many were the stories I heard of the show put up by the B.E.F., especially at Dunkirk. I can remember Yorky, a bombardier, describing the scene when the Hun crossed the Albert Canal and subsequently tried to break the British lines: British guns trapped the German infantry with a barrage to cut off their retreat, and Bren guns, ably manned by our infantry, mowed them down in thousands. When he spoke of Dunkirk he always finished up by saying, "The Germans were only trying to give us what we gave them." I heard similar comments from many others, and often wonder just what that show cost the Germans in dead and wounded; it must run into hundreds of thousands.

I made good use of my self-propelling chair, and spent many an hour talking shop with other R.A.F. pilots who were still confined to bed. Peter, a new-comer, had been transferred from another hospital, badly burnt as a result of a flying accident: he was unable to use his hands, and I assumed the role of pipe-filler and lighter – he still loved his pipe despite much pain. There was also another new member who, incidentally, was placed next to me, and I used to wheel my chair between our two beds to cope with the odd cigarette he always enjoyed.

We called him Sailor – he belonged to the Merchant Navy and had landed in a home port for the first time in two years. He had taken his father to a local tavern to celebrate the event, but unfortunately the Hun scored a direct hit on the building. Sailor's father was killed outright, and he himself received several shrapnel wounds – after only a few hours ashore. He was a typical sea salt, tough, good-natured, and possessed of an endless store of yarns. We became great friends, but Sailor was soon to go. He made a rapid recovery and

I believe he is now back at sea again. I know that the Hun will never shake him, nor will they ever match the manly qualities which he and his kind possess.

The Hun continued to drop a few bombs around the place pretty regularly, and many were the arguments which arose as to whether they were Ack-Acks or bombs. Whenever anyone suggested guns, Buster would chime in with "Famous last words those, famous last words!" He, incidentally, was the cause of much laughter one night. Bombs were falling quite near us and Buster, who had that day tried to walk for the first time with much groaning, was sitting up listening intently. The Hun dropped a stick of bombs, the first falling quite near, and the building shook; another fell nearer, and the building seemed to lift and then drop; another fell nearer still, and the beds moved.

"The next drops in here," someone said. There was a rustle of sheets and we looked towards Buster's bed; it was empty. The next bomb did not arrive, and Buster wormed his way out from under the bed to be greeted with peals of laughter. Leg or no leg, Buster had dived to safety.

A patient from another ward was brought in for the salt bath treatment; she was a young girl who had been badly burnt when the factory in which she worked was blitzed. Joan became a great favourite in the ward, and despite the burns, which would have killed many an older person, she retained her sense of humour. It is hard to believe that only a few days ago I saw Joan walking in the grounds of the hospital smiling and chatting away to friends, yet, when she first arrived, few thought she would live, let alone walk again.

One day a Royal visitor, H.R.H. the Duke of Kent, toured the hospital. He came through the ward and chatted to each patient for a few minutes. He was accompanied by 'The Maestro', Matron, the Hospital Superintendent, and many others, including members of the Hospital Committee. Sisters and nurses were presented to him; it was a great occasion.

Then came Christmas Day. The ward was decorated by the hospital staff, and kind people who lived in the neighbourhood presented a Christmas tree to which were attached many very acceptable gifts. Others gave cigarettes and a keg of beer. A concert party provided entertainment which gave zest to the festivity, and wine and song added their contribution to an enjoyable party.

1941 dawned. New Year's Day was celebrated with a concert. Speeches were made. A great man in public affairs was present; he was one of the hospital's benefactors and had just been honoured by the King. He was warmly congratulated by all, especially by those who were enjoying some of the results of his generosity. Mrs. Ceylon and the Major's wife received bouquets from grateful patients: they were two of a number who gave generously to the hospital and spent much time on our behalf; many were their kindnesses.

Old patients left; some healed, made sound again, others well enough to convalesce for a while before further treatment. New patients arrived, and amongst them came Eric, an R.A.F. pilot with a collection of Huns to his credit, and Paul, a flying pupil who had been badly burnt in a crash.

'The Maestro' came round one evening and surveyed my face.

"You need a new nose," he said. "What about it?"

I had no intention of arguing with one to whom the grafting of a complete face was no novelty, and said, "I'll do whatever you suggest."

That evening the corporal, or I should say the sergeant, for he had just been promoted, much to the deep satisfaction of all who knew him, came to my bedside armed with a pair of scissors and barber's clippers.

"I'm going to give you a monk's haircut, sir, a real bob!" he said with a grin. Within a few minutes I was 'nude' from my forehead to a point just in line with my ears. The sergeant handed me a mirror, and I perceived in my reflection a near reproduction of Friar Tuck. This unfortunate operation was necessary, as part of my forehead was to be used for the construction of my new nose. The other patients roared with laughter and so did I; the joke was on me.

Next day I was wheeled in, and came round again in the evening. Doc came to see me and said that the flap would be put back in about fourteen days.

The days passed slowly. I had one sore spot which caused me some bother, but otherwise I had little to worry about, thanks to the care taken of me by Gladys, my nurse.

I was nearing the end of my time when one or two patients were found to be suffering from some mild infection, and 'The Maestro' decided to separate the ward for a while to prevent any recurrence. Sidi Barrani, Yorky, Josef, Eric, and myself were therefore moved over to an empty ward; it had been the Maternity Ward, but production had slackened off. When I arrived there, I found that the sergeant was a fellow patient – his hands were badly chafed, due to working continuously in the salt, and he was now under treatment. Two patients arrived from other wards, Dick and John, both R.A.F. pilots.

We were to have no visitors for a few days, and Eric gave vent to his feelings by declaring that all except himself suffered from 'dog-rot' and he was bound to get it, in fact he might possibly 'give birth'. Roars of laughter greeted Eric's remarks, and several others intimated that they were feeling 'maternal'. That night Dick kept us amused by relating his adventures in Paris some years before, when he toured the sights accompanied by a friend who lived there. His descriptions of French frivolities evoked much mirth.

Next day the barber arrived. He had instructions to give all and sundry 'a healthy hair-cut'. Dick and John protested loudly. Their protests were greeted by shouts of "Take it off, barber," "Clip it short," and "Make no bones about it." They compromised, both having enough off to claim 'a haircut', though it was hard to notice the fact. When Sidi Barrani's turn came round, the barber received encouragement from all quarters. Sidi had a long black mop of hair which Eric suggested was the cause of the dog-rot and encouraged the barber to further efforts.

One morning when I awoke there was great activity in the ward. The Hun had been bombing that night, and a large bomb, weighing over a ton, had dropped in a field nearby – unexploded. They were evacuating our ward as we were the nearest to it. I was having my flap put back that day, and when I came-to again I was back in my old ward. I now had the material for my new nose in position, and it was just a matter of trimming once it had settled down.

In a few days I was feeling grand, grand enough to try to take my weight on my feet, and with the help of a bed-table I was soon staggering from pillar to pillar unaided.

The Major took me out in his car, and I again saw country lanes, trees, and grassland. To some this may seem trivial, but to those who have spent many months in bed or within the confines of a ward it is a great thrill and a fine tonic. The Major was one of those people who, out of kindness of heart, spent whatever time he could afford in visiting the patients and taking them out for drives in the country. There are many who remember him with gratitude.

Then the great day dawned: I was to go on sick-leave down to the South Coast to be with my family again. My wife came to help me cope with station steps and carriage doors, and I bade goodbye to my fellow patients. Sidi Barrani and Yorky were shortly going out for good, the latter having been discharged from the Army as totally unfit, I was sorry to see the last of those two grand fellows.

For a month I practised the art of walking and then returned for a Medical Board.

Neville, Jack, and Poley Boy were down at Torquay, and Josef was somewhere up North convalescing. Paul was still there and likely to be for many a long day; he had just had a large piece of skin lifted from his stomach to form a pedicle, preparatory to receiving a new face. He was a stout fellow and never complained – a perfect answer,

THE RED CROSS

one of millions, to the gangsters and coarse-throated bull-frogs of Europe who once proclaimed the 'decadence of British youth'.

Eric had just had another 'op', and was coming round when I arrived. He was giving a lecture on grafts, and suggested that if his latest patch didn't take, then riveting should be resorted to. He also discoursed on the 'treatment of dog-rot', and finally came-to.

"How do, Squad, how's the nose?" he asked.

Grand, I replied, and sat down to talk more shop with him.

I had arrived in time to see Peter wheeled out into the sun once again. He was now making progress, and it was good to see him finding new life after so much suffering. I looked around for Perky, but heard he was away for a few weeks.

Next day I was boarded in the presence of George, an R.A.F. surgeon I had known years before and who had recently arrived at the hospital; he was a great fellow and a fine surgeon by repute. I was ordered to go off for another month, and away I went.

I could now walk quite well, and started to move in ever-widening circles. I visited a local aerodrome and met some old friends, old pupils of mine, amongst whom were Nigel and Peggy of flying training days. They were doing well and hoping that the Hun would oblige with another 'Armada' like last autumn. Then they were smashed and scattered; next time they will be massacred, annihilated.

At night I used sometimes to stand in the garden watching the firework display put up by the anti-aircraft guns protecting the local dockyard. I would hear the drone of the Hun and then another sound, the engine of a fighter on his track. Many times, I heard cannon and machine-gun fire, but although several Huns fell in the vicinity, I always seemed to miss the spectacle.

By day I watched the fighters going off on patrol or to intercept a raider. New Spitfires, new Hurricanes, Beaufighters, and occasionally a Havoc flew overhead. It was good to see them; I felt I was still in touch with flying.

I HAD A ROW WITH A GERMAN

One morning a letter arrived from 'Somewhere in the North'. It was from my old Squadron, and in it I read of their record in the Battle of Britain. They had shot down approximately forty confirmed, and sixteen probably destroyed, besides many others damaged. Though I have done little in this war, I feel proud that, in my own small way, I have been associated with them. I read too, with much regret, that, in addition to Star, Jenks, and Dicky, Bill, Curly, the Air Commodore, and Sammy have now been killed, and that the 'Group Captain', 'Bell-Pusher' and one of the sergeants have been wounded. Bruno and others have been posted elsewhere, and Corky and Henry alone remain as representatives of the old guard. I hope I shall run across them one day in the near future, perhaps at the reunion we so often mooted.

Once again, I journeyed back to hospital. I had to wait a few days for my next 'op', and stayed a week-end with some kind people nearby who had turned their country house into a convalescent home and were themselves living in one of the wings. I enjoyed that stay very much, wandering around the grounds, visiting the racing stud, greyhound kennels, and poultry farm, and I found much to interest me. At length it was time to go back, and once again I was wheeled in and lifted on to 'the slab', and the left side of my nose was shaped.

After a few days I was out again for a while, but later I returned for still more trimming.

Perky was back, so were Poley Boy and Josef, all looking very well but with still a long way to go before leaving the hospital for good. Eric had left, and was soon going back to duty. Peter greeted me with a broad grin. He told me that a few days earlier the orderlies had dressed him up in his uniform for the first time since his crash, and he had been taken by friends to London. After much festivity he had been lifted on to a fire-engine and driven through the streets of the City accompanied by much 'playing of bells'. He seemed a different man now that he was fast becoming mobile. Few things had cheered me more than this for a long time; I admired Peter; he had been very patient. He, like Perky, had badly burnt hands – the fingers were bent almost double – and little could be done for them.

I visited Colonel Stanley and his wife; they lived nearby and had thrown their house open to us whenever we could visit or stay with them, and their hospitality was very much appreciated by us all. I had my 'op', and in a few days was off South again to let my new grafts settle down.

It was then that I started to write this book.

Chapter 4

The White Cross

A few more weeks and I shall be back on duty with a new face, strong limbs, and new life.   A few more months and I shall be flying again.

I shall soon have to say goodbye to 'The Maestro'; how to thank him I do not know. I must say goodbye to George, Doc, Matron, Sister, and the nurses; I shall have to thank them too; how, God alone knows.

Twelve months have passed, a small fraction of one's life; yet, in those twelve months I have learnt new values, felt new emotions, known a little of that side of life which the fit and strong rarely witness. I have gained imperishable memories of devoted and courageous men and women who live to save and mend what others seek to destroy. I know my debt to them, immeasurable though it be, but I have other debts, and in these I am not alone.

Sentiment and pathos may have little place in our lives in times of peace, perhaps less in times of war; but we should be denying ourselves the prerogative of humans if we failed to feel emotion at the sacrifice of others for our benefit.

There can be few of us who cannot recall some acquaintance, some face we knew well, now turned to a mere memory by death. To them we owe a debt, all of us, and we can only hope to repay some of it by striving to achieve that sense of values and that unselfish standard of human intercourse for which they fought and died, and without which we can never hope to know a better world.

And what of those who offered no less, yet still survive, maimed and crippled, shorn of some of their faculties or those physical abilities which make life complete? They remain, and we are their trustees.

We owe them no less a debt. Must they, like many of their counterparts of a generation ago, know poverty and feel the soul-searing torment of grudging charity? Must they be victims of life's most vicious crime – man's ingratitude to man?

To them the charity that maintains existence, however well-intentioned the source, is not enough. They must do more than exist; they must live.

Many men sympathise with their physical loss, but few realise perhaps that one can lose no faculty or ability without that loss affecting something more than just the body. To men of rational and intelligent minds the will to justify one's existence, to take a place in the scheme of things and hold an honoured position in the community of men, however humble, holds a higher place than any other. To say "You have done your bit" means little to one to whom a monotonous existence brings torture of the soul far greater than torture of the body.

It is to us, therefore, that they look for the opportunities and facilities which will give them life. We must provide the workshops, the homes, and those requirements whereby the blind, the maimed, and the crippled may put to useful purpose the faculties and physical abilities they still retain. Many of them may make their employment profitable, others may not; but the fact that they are making a contribution, however small, towards the varied needs of the community will give them a peace of mind and a feeling of accomplishment far transcending the vacant existence of mind and soul which well-intentioned but soul-destroying charity can only produce.

They came from many walks of life, but those which are foremost in my mind are my fellow men of the Royal Air Force. May they know and feel again the true warmth of a life they once knew. May we, in the aftermath of 'this our finest hour', keep our sacred trust.

Acknowledgements

The author acknowledges with gratitude the help and advice he received from the Air Ministry in the final preparation of the script. Without their sanction this book could not have been published. His thanks are also due to Air Vice-Marshal T. Leigh-Mallory, C.B., D.S.O., who so kindly wrote the Foreword.

He desires to place on record his grateful thanks to the Ministry of Information and others through whose kind permission the reproduction of various illustrations included in this book was possible.

In conclusion, he proffers his humble thanks to all those of diverse professions who took, and still take, a great personal interest in the welfare of Service wounded, often forgoing well-deserved rest in order to entertain and cheer them up, and who so kindly sent their messages of good luck to "I had a row with a German",

The Author

PART III

AFTER PUBLICATION

AFTER PUBLICATION

```
                                                    Jill
        Telephones:              HEADQUARTERS,
     Ramsgate 196 & 197       ROYAL AIR FORCE STATION,
      Telegraphic Address:      MANSTON, Nr. RAMSGATE,
    " Aeronautics, Ramsgate."                           KENT.
   Reference No.:— DO/T.P.G.
                                12th December, 1941.


            Dear A.V.M.

                    I enclose herewith a copy of my book which please accept
            with my grateful thanks for the Foreword and the kind interest you have
            displayed in its production.

                    You will note that the title has been changed, and that
            some of the photographs have been excluded.  The former was agreed
            to on the advice of the Publisher's readers who are very experienced
            and know what is attractive to the public, and the latter is due to the
            universal shortage of photographic paper.

                    I sincerely hope you will enjoy reading it a second
            time now that it has been cleaned up and tidied in a few places.

                                Yours

         Air Vice-Marshal T.L.Leigh-Mallory, C.B.,D.S.O.
         Headquarters, No.11 Group,
         Uxbridge, Midd.
```

No sooner had Tom received some of his copies of his book, then he began sending them out with covering notes for each recipient. One of the first individuals he wrote to, on 12 December 1941, the same day that *I Had a Row With a German* was officially published by Macmillan & Co, was Air Vice-Marshal Leigh-Mallory at RAF Uxbridge.

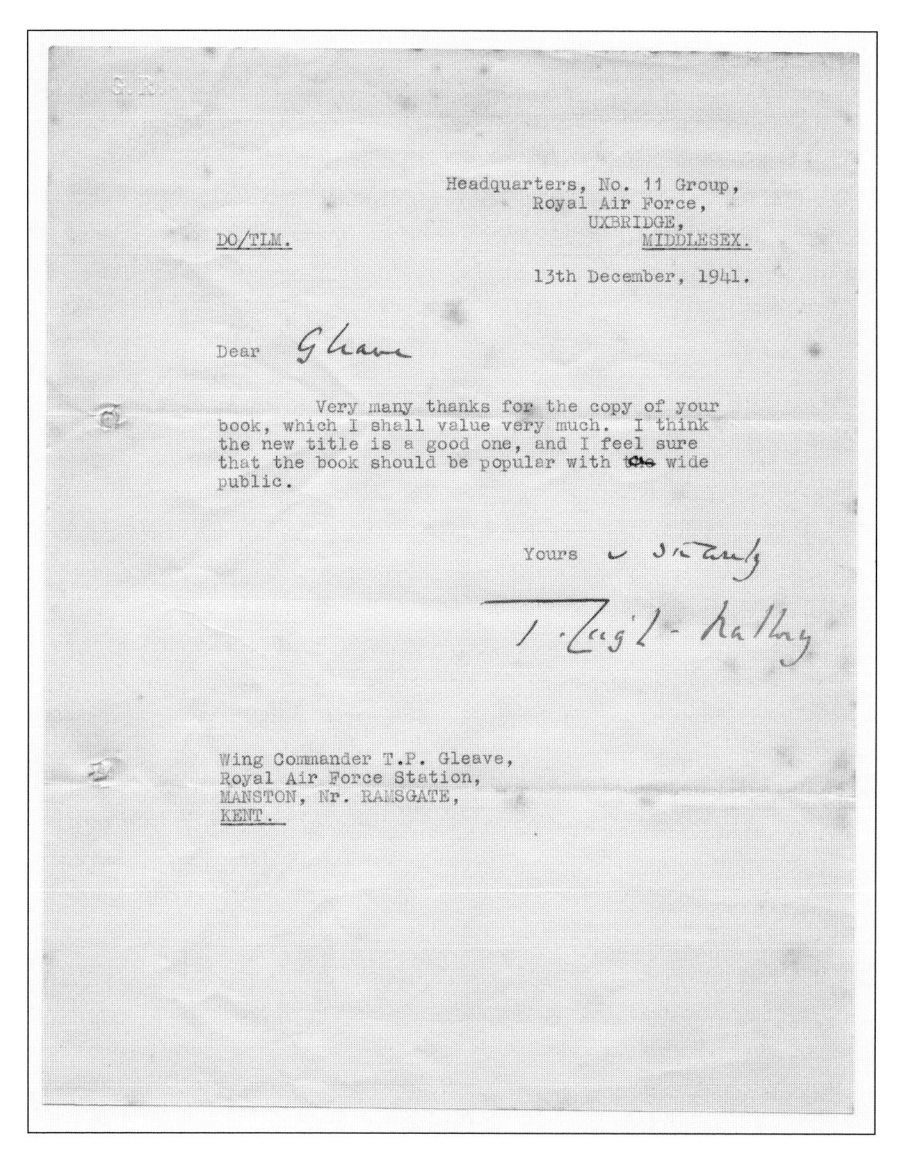

> Headquarters, No. 11 Group,
> Royal Air Force,
> UXBRIDGE,
> MIDDLESEX.
>
> DO/TLM.
>
> 13th December, 1941.
>
> Dear Gleave
>
> Very many thanks for the copy of your book, which I shall value very much. I think the new title is a good one, and I feel sure that the book should be popular with the wide public.
>
> Yours sincerely
> T. Leigh-Mallory
>
> Wing Commander T.P. Gleave,
> Royal Air Force Station,
> MANSTON, Nr. RAMSGATE,
> KENT.

Having received his copy of the book, Air Vice-Marshal Leigh-Mallory promptly acknowledged its arrival the very next day, 13 December 1941. In doing so, Leigh-Mallory was one of the first people to congratulate Tom on his achievements.

AFTER PUBLICATION

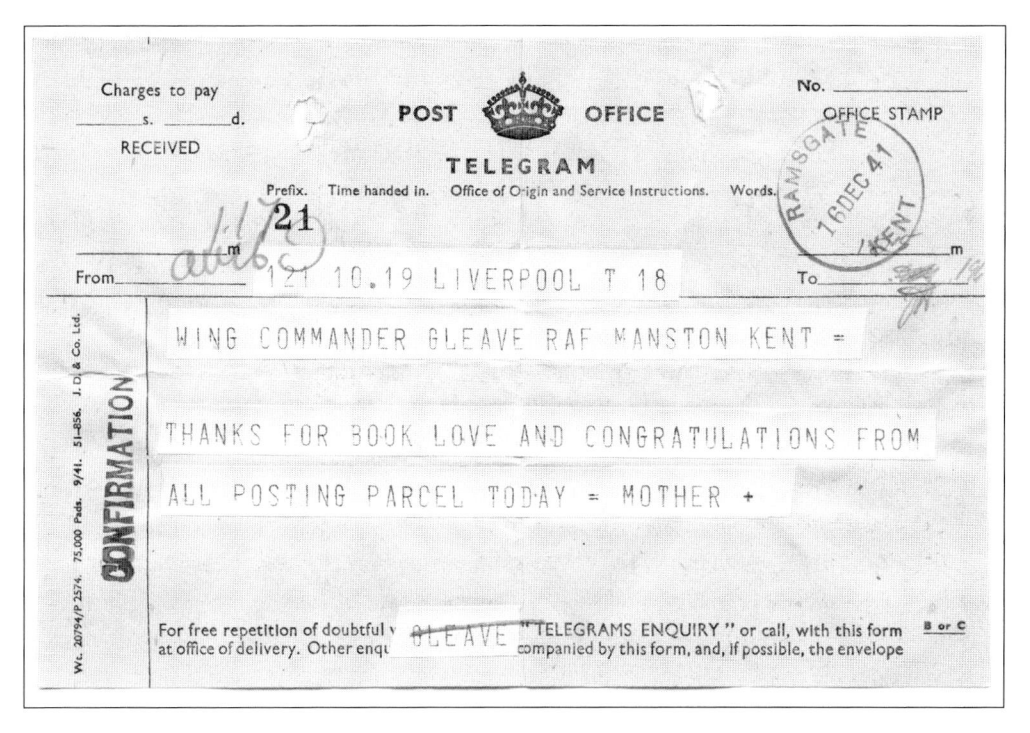

The telegram from Tom Gleave's mother congratulating him on the book, copies of which had been received at the family home. It arrived at RAF Manston on 16 December 1941.

I HAD A ROW WITH A GERMAN

```
TELEGRAMS: "PUBLISH, LESQUARE, LONDON"         MACMILLAN & CO. LTD.
CABLES: "PUBLISH, LONDON"
TELEPHONE: WHITEHALL 8831                         ST. MARTIN'S STREET,
CODE: 5TH AND 6TH EDITIONS A.B.C                  LONDON, W.C.2.

PLEASE QUOTE LD/JS                                30th January, 1942.
```

Wing-Commander T. P. Gleave,
Officers' Mess,
Doone House,
Westgate, East Kent.

Dear Wing Commander Gleave,

    I enclose a paste-up of a prospectus we intend to issue for I HAD A ROW WITH A GERMAN. Will you let me know if it has your approval? We should also like to know how many copies you could distribute, and whether you can suggest any names to which the prospectus can be sent.

    Your letter of January 28th has just come in. We have noted the details of the five hundred copies, and these will go off as soon as possible.

    I shall be very glad indeed to have lunch with you next time you are in London. Perhaps you will telephone me and fix a time.

    Yours sincerely,

    Lovat Dickson.

Enclosure

On 30 January 1942, Lovat Dickson typed a letter to Tom Gleave and enclosed a sample of a promotional leaflet that was to be printed.

AFTER PUBLICATION

The front of the promotional leaflet for *I Had a Row With a German*. It is based on a cartoon by Tom Webster – but not the one that Tom Gleave retained in his archive.

TITLE

"What on earth have you been doing with yourself, darling?"

"Had a row with a German."

Thus the R.A.F. fighter pilot, dreadfully burned after being shot down during the Battle of Britain, to his wife when she visited him for the first time in hospital.

"R.A.F. Casualty" covers the identity of one among the matchless few whose heroism was given tribute in Mr. Churchill's memorable sentence in Parliament. "R.A.F. Casualty's" story, which goes from the outbreak of war to the moment when he crashed in flames, is told without emphasis and with entire modesty, but it is so gallant a story that it must touch everybody's heart and arouse everyone's interest.

REVIEWS

"The book is well worth reading if only because it shows the qualities of modesty and courage which seem to be inherent in R.A.F. men." *Times Literary Supplement.*

"Few men can have had narrower escapes than the "R.A.F. Casualty" who writes it; few could describe it as well."

Reynolds News.

"Not the least attractive feature of his book is the quite unconscious picture that it paints of genuine modesty and undramatised heroism." *Sunday Times.*

"A readable and exciting set of personal impressions, well illustrated." *Daily Sketch.*

ORDER FORM

To ....(Booksellers)

....

Please send me a copy of I HAD A ROW WITH A GERMAN, by R.A.F. CASUALTY.   5s. net.

Name ....

Address ....

At the Author's request, all the royalties earned by the sale of this book are to be given to the R.A.F. Benevolent Fund

The rear of Macmillan & Co.'s promotional leaflet.

> Officers' Mess,
> Royal Air Force,
> Doone House,
> Westgate-on-Sea,
> East Kent.
> 31st January, 1942.
>
> Dear Mr. Lovat Dickson,
>
> I am returning herewith your knock-up of the prospectus. I think it is excellent, and so far as I am concerned, I fully approve of it. I have written a letter to Mr. Tom Webster, telling him why it could not be produced in the book proper, but how it is intended to be printed in the prospectus form. I have asked him to drop me a line, or send me a wire, saying that he agrees to this. I do not think he will raise any objection, so I think it quite safe to presume that we can proceed as you intend.
>
> Regarding my quota, it is quite possible I shall want another lot later, but I will let you know when I see you next.
>
> I have heard from my people and relatives, and I hear that the book is in big demand on Merseyside, and also that permission has been asked by several people for my name to be published in certain papers. This is

Regarding the design of the promotional leaflet, Tom replied positively to Lovat Dickson the next day – 31 January 1942. This is the front side of that letter.

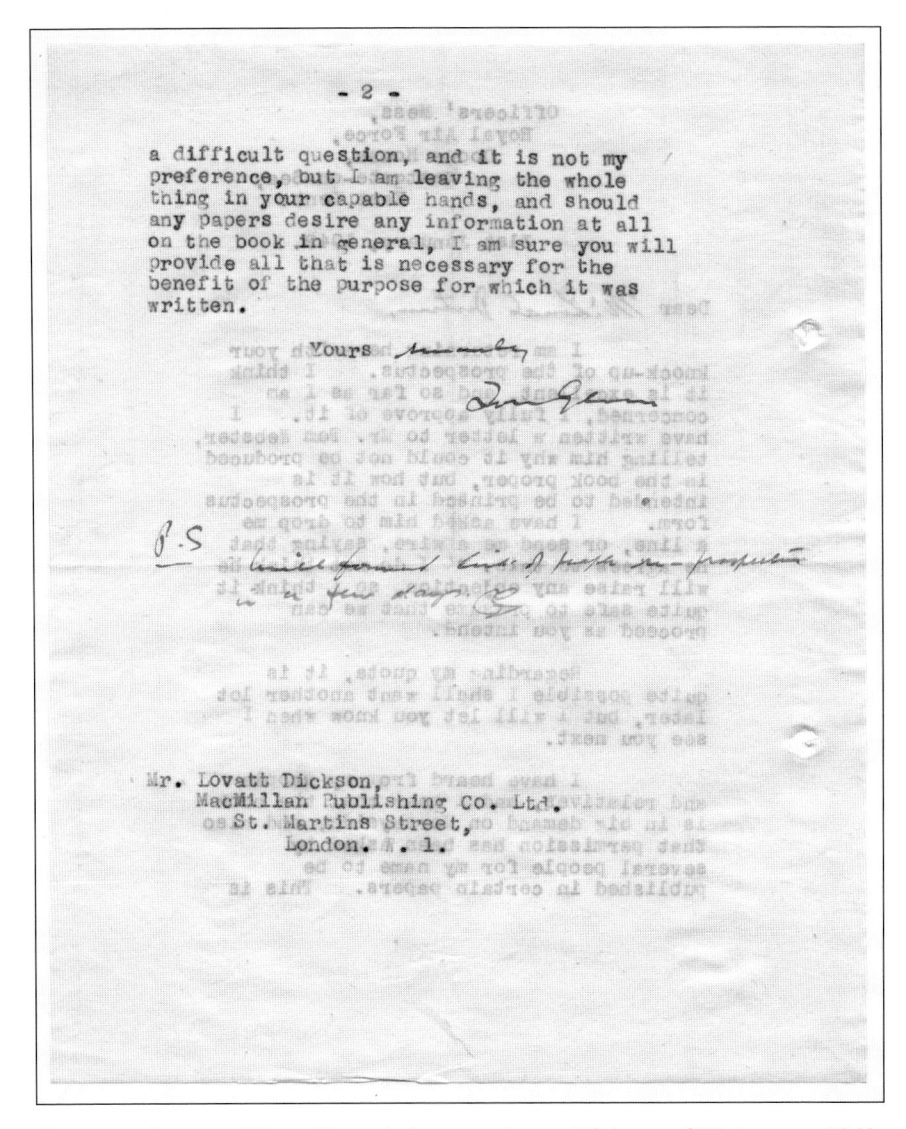

> - 2 -
>
> a difficult question, and it is not my
> preference, but I am leaving the whole
> thing in your capable hands, and should
> any papers desire any information at all
> on the book in general, I am sure you will
> provide all that is necessary for the
> benefit of the purpose for which it was
> written.
>
> Yours *[signature]*
>
> P.S. *[handwritten postscript]*
>
> Mr. Lovatt Dickson,
> MacMillan Publishing Co. Ltd.,
> St. Martins Street,
> London.

The second page of Tom Gleave's letter to Lovat Dickson of 31 January 1942. As can be seen, Tom has raised the question of his anonymity: 'I hear that the book is in big demand on Merseyside, and also that permission has been asked by several people for my name to be published in certain papers. This is a difficult question, and it is not my preference, but I am leaving the whole thing in your capable hands.'

AFTER PUBLICATION

> Officers' Mess,
> Royal Air Force,
> Doone House,
> Westgate-on-Sea,
> East Kent.
>
> 31st January, 1942.
>
> Dear [handwritten],
>
> My book, originally titled 'Eagles of Nemesis', has now been published under the title "I had a row with a German". Unfortunately, due to reproduction difficulties, the limited number of illustrations that could be included - approximately only 20% of the original number - and fitting into text, it was not possible to include your excellent cartoon actually in the book; but the publishers have drawn up an excellent prospectus to go with the book, with your cartoon reproduced thereon as the main attraction, and they have submitted a knock-up for my approval. Personally, I think it is excellent, but was anxious to let you know how it is being reproduced. The publishers intend running off a considerable number of these, and I am forwarding to them a long list of people to whom they are to be sent. I presume, of course, that they will be used as an advertisement on a large scale.
>
> The first edition was sold

Tom Gleave wrote to Tom Webster on 31 January 1942, informing him that whilst his cartoon could not be included in the book after all, it was to be used on the promotional leaflet that Macmillan & Co. were planning to produce.

- 2 -

out on the day of publication, and a second edition has just come through. I hope, therefore, to receive my quota in a few days; I shall then forward one to you, which I hope you will please accept for your great kindness to me and to our efforts for the Royal Air Force Benevolent Fund.

I shall be very grateful if you will drop me a line, or send me a wire, saying you agree to the form of reproduction referred to above, so that it can be run off and published as soon as possible.

If you have no objection, I am very keen to keep the original myself as a memento of the book, as I take it one of the highest compliments paid to the Service that I have seen in the form of a cartoon picture, or anything else.

Hoping I shall have the pleasure of seeing you again soon.

Yours

Wing Commander,
Royal Air Force.

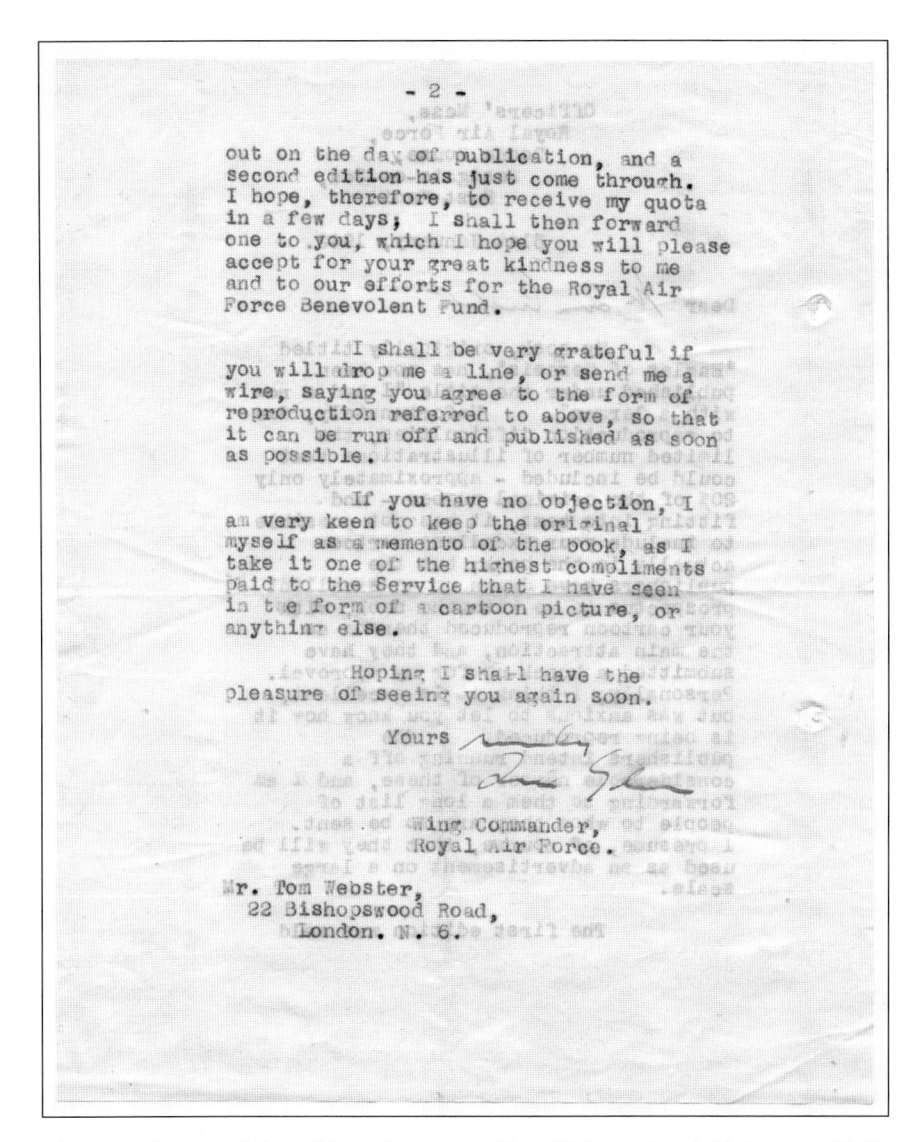

Mr. Tom Webster,
22 Bishopswood Road,
London. N. 6.

The second page of Tom Gleave's letter to Tom Webster dated 31 January 1942. Interestingly, in the letter Tom points out that the first edition of the book was sold out on the day of publication. A second edition was hastily printed.

AFTER PUBLICATION

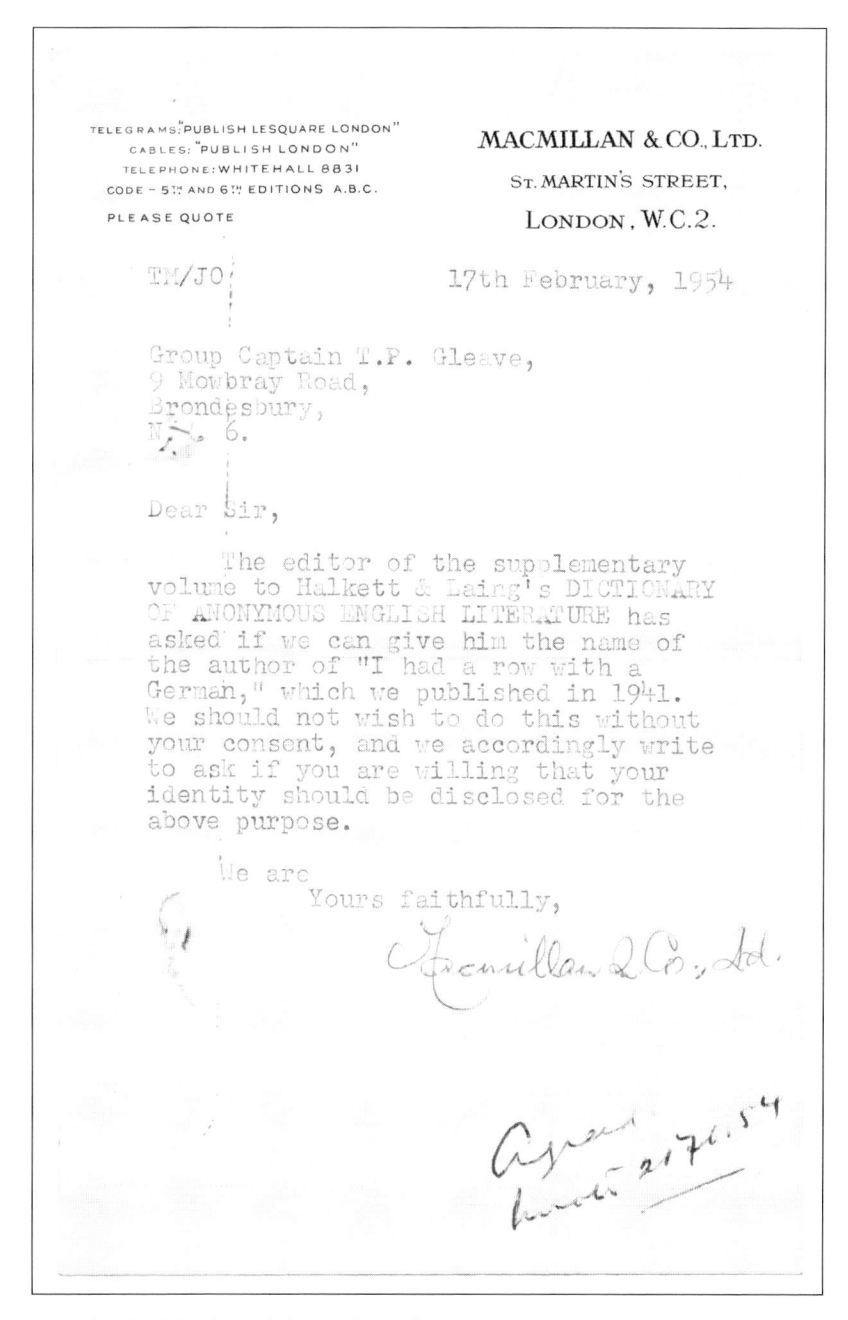

> TELEGRAMS: "PUBLISH LESQUARE LONDON"
> CABLES: "PUBLISH LONDON"
> TELEPHONE: WHITEHALL 8831
> CODE - 5TH AND 6TH EDITIONS A.B.C.
>
> PLEASE QUOTE
>
> MACMILLAN & CO., LTD.
> ST. MARTIN'S STREET,
> LONDON, W.C.2.
>
> TM/JO
>
> 17th February, 1954
>
> Group Captain T.P. Gleave,
> 9 Mowbray Road,
> Brondesbury,
> N.W. 6.
>
> Dear Sir,
>
> The editor of the supplementary volume to Halkett & Laing's DICTIONARY OF ANONYMOUS ENGLISH LITERATURE has asked if we can give him the name of the author of "I had a row with a German," which we published in 1941. We should not wish to do this without your consent, and we accordingly write to ask if you are willing that your identity should be disclosed for the above purpose.
>
> We are
> Yours faithfully,
> Macmillan & Co., Ltd.

Interest in the identity of the author of *I Had a Row With a German* seemingly persisted. On 17 February 1954, for example, a member of staff at Macmillan & Co. wrote to Gleave with details of another request for his name to be made public. As the hand-written note bottom-right indicates, Tom agreed to the enquiry.

113

I HAD A ROW WITH A GERMAN

> MACMILLAN & CO. LTD.
> ST MARTIN'S STREET,
> LONDON, W.C.2.
>
> 3rd February, 1942.
>
> LD/JS
>
> Wing-Commander T. P. Gleave,
> Officers' Mess,
> Royal Air Force,
> Doone House,
> Westgate-on-Sea, East Kent.
>
> Dear Commander Gleave,
>
> Thank you for your letter. I am so glad that you liked the layout of the prospectus. We are going ahead with the printing of this now.
>
> I think in a way it would be a shame to break the anonymity, but if you like to leave it to us, we will decide as each request arises as to whether it is worth letting them have your name. I am glad to know that we may do so if the circumstances in any particular case look as though it would be helpful to give your name away.
>
> A problem has arisen concerning the 500 copies of your book. We are able to supply you, as the author, with copies at one-third off the list price, but cannot supply others on the same terms. Would it be in order to send the books to the names on your list, and to send the invoice to you? Otherwise we should have to invoice the copies for Mr. Arthur Gleave and Captain Banham at full list-price.
>
> Yours sincerely,
>
> Lovat Dickson.

A reply that Lovat Dickson sent in response to a previous letter from Tom. It touches on the continuing matter of anonymity, and well as further author copies.

AFTER PUBLICATION

This letter from Bertram T. Rumble at the RAF Benevolent Fund, which is dated 27 February 1942, is another that acknowledges receipt of a complimentary copy of the book.

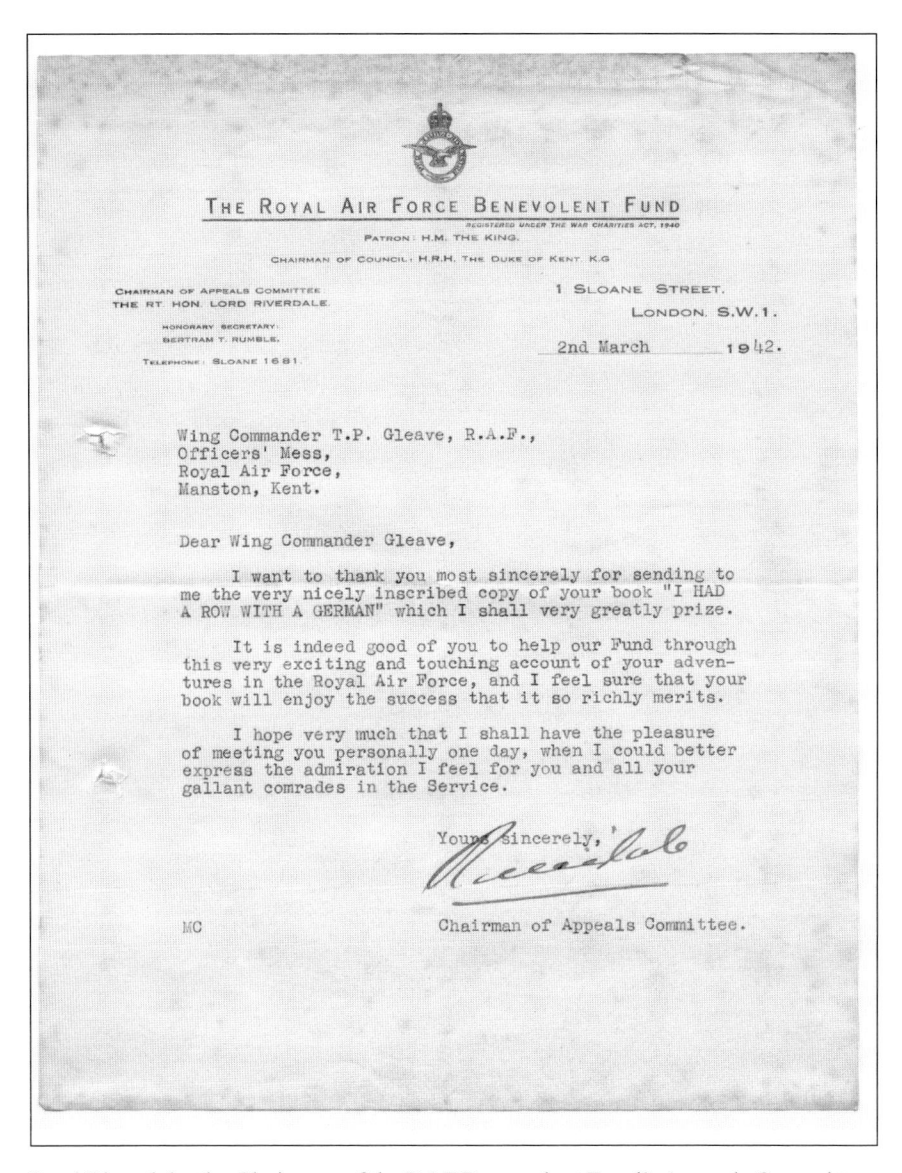

I HAD A ROW WITH A GERMAN

> **THE ROYAL AIR FORCE BENEVOLENT FUND**
> REGISTERED UNDER THE WAR CHARITIES ACT, 1940
> PATRON: H.M. THE KING.
> CHAIRMAN OF COUNCIL: H.R.H. THE DUKE OF KENT. K.G
>
> CHAIRMAN OF APPEALS COMMITTEE
> THE RT. HON. LORD RIVERDALE.
> HONORARY SECRETARY:
> BERTRAM T. RUMBLE.
> TELEPHONE: SLOANE 1681.
>
> 1 SLOANE STREET,
> LONDON. S.W.1.
>
> 2nd March 1942.
>
> Wing Commander T.P. Gleave, R.A.F.,
> Officers' Mess,
> Royal Air Force,
> Manston, Kent.
>
> Dear Wing Commander Gleave,
>
> I want to thank you most sincerely for sending to me the very nicely inscribed copy of your book "I HAD A ROW WITH A GERMAN" which I shall very greatly prize.
>
> It is indeed good of you to help our Fund through this very exciting and touching account of your adventures in the Royal Air Force, and I feel sure that your book will enjoy the success that it so richly merits.
>
> I hope very much that I shall have the pleasure of meeting you personally one day, when I could better express the admiration I feel for you and all your gallant comrades in the Service.
>
> Yours sincerely,
>
> *Riverdale*
>
> Chairman of Appeals Committee.
>
> MC

Lord Riverdale, the Chairman of the RAF Benevolent Fund's Appeals Committee, followed up Rumble's communication to Tom with this letter that is dated 2 March 1942.

AFTER PUBLICATION

> HEADQUARTERS, FIGHTER COMMAND,
> ROYAL AIR FORCE,
> BENTLEY PRIORY,
> STANMORE,
> MIDDLESEX.
>
> TEL: WATFORD 3241.
>
> 9th March 1942.
>
> Dear *Wing Commander*
>
> The C.-in-C. has asked me to thank you very much indeed for the copy of your book "I Had a Row with a German", and to tell you that he is looking forward to reading it.
>
> The C.-in-C. also asked me to express his appreciation of the fact that all the proceeds from the sale of this book are going to the benefit of the Royal Air Force Benevolent Fund, in which, as you know, he takes a very great interest.
>
> Yours sincerely,
>
> *[signature]*
>
> Flight Lieutenant,
> Personal Assistant to A.O.C.-in-C.
>
> Wing Commander T.P. Gleave,
>   Royal Air Force,
>   Manston,
>   Kent.

One of the complimentary copies that Tom Gleave sent out was to Air Marshal Sholto Douglas. As the Commander-in-Chief of Fighter Command, Douglas was based at RAF Bentley Priory near Stanmore, Middlesex. Receipt of this copy was acknowledged by Douglas' Personal Assistant in this note of 9 March 1942.

I HAD A ROW WITH A GERMAN

> HEADQUARTERS, FIGHTER COMMAND,
> ROYAL AIR FORCE,
> BENTLEY PRIORY,
> STANMORE,
> MIDDLESEX.
>
> 11th March 1942.
>
> My dear Gleave -
>
> I have just finished reading your book, which I enjoyed immensely. The middle part, in which you describe your combat experiences, is particularly vivid and well written.
>
> Thank you very much indeed for sending me a copy, which I shall treasure in my book-case.
>
> Yours sincerely,
> Sholto Douglas
>
> Wing Commander T.P. Gleave,
>   Royal Air Force Station,
>   Manston,
>   Near Ramsgate, Kent.

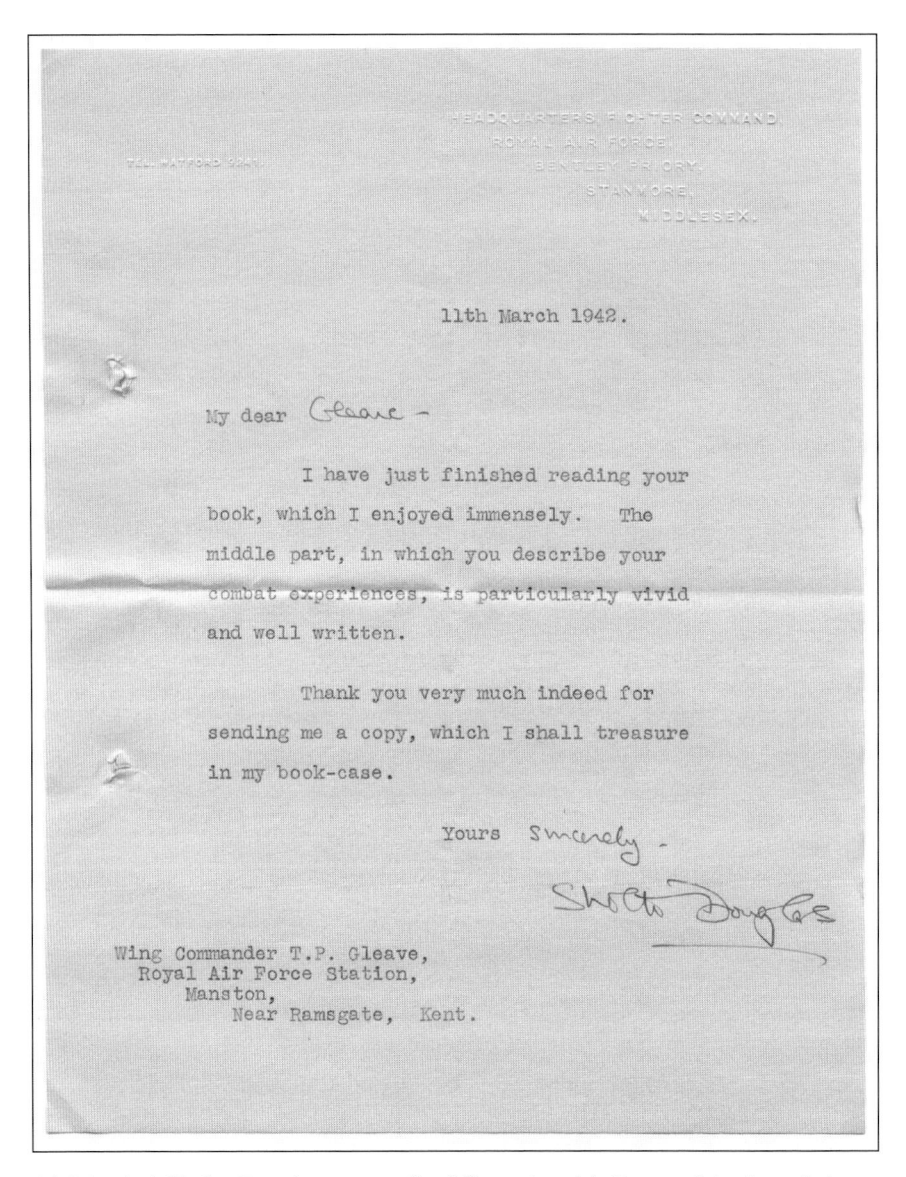

Air Marshal Sholto Douglas personally followed up his Personal Assistant's letter two days later on 11 March 1942.

AFTER PUBLICATION

CITY OF LIVERPOOL

FROM
THE HEADMASTER
TEL. ANFIELD 613

LIVERPOOL COLLEGIATE SCHOOL
LIVERPOOL, 6

KAC/DMM   20th March, 1942.

Dear Mr. Gleave,

   Thank you very much for your book which I have placed in the School Library. We shall be proud to have it. I am distributing the leaflets you sent me.

   With best wishes.

      Yours sincerely,

         Ka Crofts

         Acting Headmaster.

T.P. Gleave Esq.
Officers' Mess.
Royal Air Force.
Doone House,
Westgate-on-Sea,
Kent.

One of Tom Gleave's old schools, in this case Liverpool Collegiate School, acknowledged receipt of their complimentary copy of the book on 20 March 1942.

> Mace Farm.
> Cudham.
> Nr. Sevenoaks
> Kent.
> 26.3.42.
>
> Dear Mr Gleave,
>
> Many thanks indeed for your great kindness in sending me a copy of your very interesting book. I feel very honoured to have come into it & I really did so very little for you after all you & many others have done for us.
>
> Without you & your wonderful colleagues this little island of ours would have been a sad place today. I have been long in acknowledg

On 26 March 1942, Tom Gleave received a letter from Constance Wilson of Mace Farm, Cudham, Kent – where his aircraft crashed on that fateful August day in 1940.

> 2
>
> your book, we left Scotland in January after being away from home 16 months. It is a great joy to be all together again & we hope we were right in our decision to bring the children back again into this area, but we felt we could not go on indefinitely away from home. A farm needs someone on the spot.
>
> I am amazed to think you remembered everything so clearly, no you did not get handy I felt you were anxious not to, we moistened your lips with Sal-volatile & gave you a cup of tea & glucose.
>
> Had I known there you could

The second page of the letter from Constance Wilson of Mace Farm. It contains the following: 'I really did so very little for you after all you and many others have done for us. Without you and your wonderful colleagues this little island of ours would have been a sad place today.'

I HAD A ROW WITH A GERMAN

have got into a car I could have taken you straight away to Orpington, but probably the rest did help a little.
I hope your book has a big sale & may you enjoy all you richly deserve.
We hope to meet you one day & if ever you are near & need somewhere for your wife & little son we would always try to put them or yourself up here.
Again many thanks
Yours sincerely
Constance E. Wilson

The third and last page of Constance Wilson's letter.

AFTER PUBLICATION

```
TELEGRAMS: "PUBLISH, LESQUARE, LONDON"      MACMILLAN & CO. LTD.
    CABLES: "PUBLISH, LONDON"
    TELEPHONE: WHITEHALL 8831                ST. MARTIN'S STREET,
    CODE: 5TH AND 6TH EDITIONS A.B.C
                                             LONDON, W.C.2.

    PLEASE QUOTE  LD/VP               1st April, 1942.
```

Wing-Commander T.P. Gleave,
Headquarters,
R.A.F. Station,
Manston, Kent.

Dear Gleave,

    Thank you for your letter of March 31st, and for your cheque for £84 1s. 8d. The book is continuing to go very well. We have sold 5,700 to date, so you have made a very remarkable individual contribution to the R.A.F. Benevolent Fund.

    I hope you are going to come up soon and have lunch with me

               Yours sincerely,

               Lovat Dickson.

Enclosure:

On 1 April 1942, Lovat Dickson wrote to Tom to inform him that 5,700 copies of the book had already been sold.

I HAD A ROW WITH A GERMAN

A letter that Tom received from a reader which is dated 4 April 1942. The writer made the following comment: 'I have one criticism to make – it is too short!'

AFTER PUBLICATION

> Tel. No. 666
>
> **The Maxillo Facial Unit**
> OF
> **Queen Victoria Cottage Hospital**
> East Grinstead
>
> MP/4/9.
>
> HOLTYE ROAD
>
> SECRETARY-SUPERINTENDENT
> W. J. BANHAM
> A.H.O.A.
>
> 7th April, 1942.
>
> Dear Gleave,
>
> Herewith a further cheque for £2.10. 0d. being the balance due in respect of the 50 copies of your book.
>
> I asked Archie about the twelve you gave to the Hospital and he says he has received them and will write you.
>
> If you want me to sell any more and care to send me some I will do my best to dispose of them.
>
> Yours sincerely,
>
> *W J Banham*
>
> Secretary-Superintendent.
>
> Wing Commander T. Gleave,
> Headquarters,
> Royal Air Force Station,
> Manston,
> Nr. Ramsgate,
> Kent.
>
> P.S. I should welcome an autographed copy if you feel so inclined — All the best W.J.B.

Tom never forgot those who had helped him in the aftermath of being shot down in August 1940. Dated 7 April 1942, this letter from the Secretary-Superintendent of the Queen Victoria Cottage Hospital in East Grinstead is thanking him for a batch of his books that he had sent them. Note the reference to McIndoe.

> Orpington War Hospital,
> Orpington,
> Kent.
>
> 8th April, 1942.
>
> Dear Group Captain Gleave,
>
> Thank you very much for the further batch of your books. I have put some in the wards and the remainder in the hospital library so that they will be available for all wards. I have also put two in the Nurses' Home which I thought would be agreeable to your wishes.
>
> May I say again how much I enjoyed the book and it is a great pleasure to see someone like yourself writing *as you have* about the hospital and nurses and a great encouragement in their work.
>
> Yours sincerely,
>
> Maurice Campbell
>
> Medical Superintendent.

The Orpington War Hospital received the same treatment from Tom as the Queen Victoria Cottage Hospital. This letter from the Medical Superintendent at Orpington War Hospital is thanking him for a supply of the books that Tom had donated.

AFTER PUBLICATION

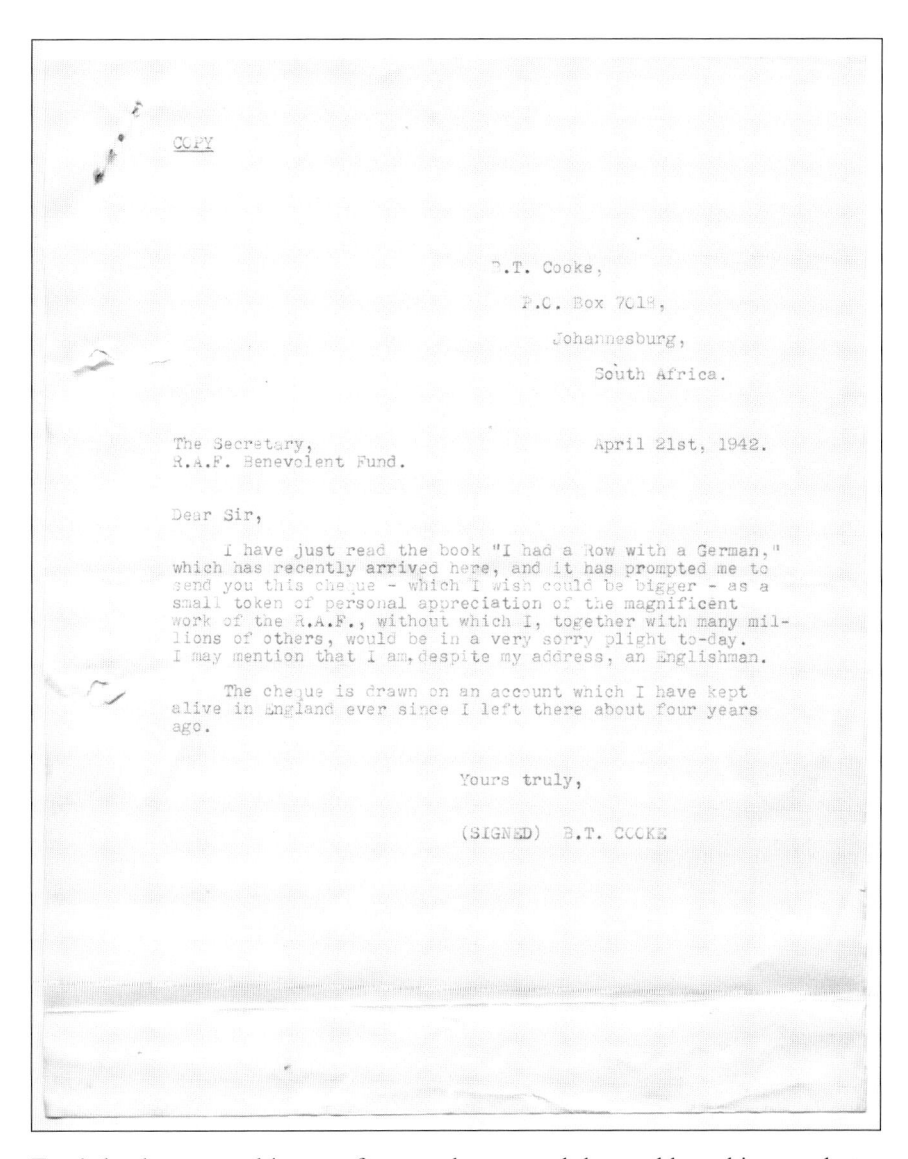

> COPY
>
>   B.T. Cooke,
>   P.O. Box 7018,
>   Johannesburg,
>   South Africa.
>
> The Secretary,   April 21st, 1942.
> R.A.F. Benevolent Fund.
>
> Dear Sir,
>
>   I have just read the book "I had a Row with a German," which has recently arrived here, and it has prompted me to send you this cheque - which I wish could be bigger - as a small token of personal appreciation of the magnificent work of the R.A.F., without which I, together with many millions of others, would be in a very sorry plight to-day. I may mention that I am, despite my address, an Englishman.
>
>   The cheque is drawn on an account which I have kept alive in England ever since I left there about four years ago.
>
>   Yours truly,
>
>   (SIGNED) B.T. COOKE

Tom's book generated interest from readers around the world, as this copy letter, dated 21 April 1942, which arrived with a donation from South Africa, indicates.

I HAD A ROW WITH A GERMAN

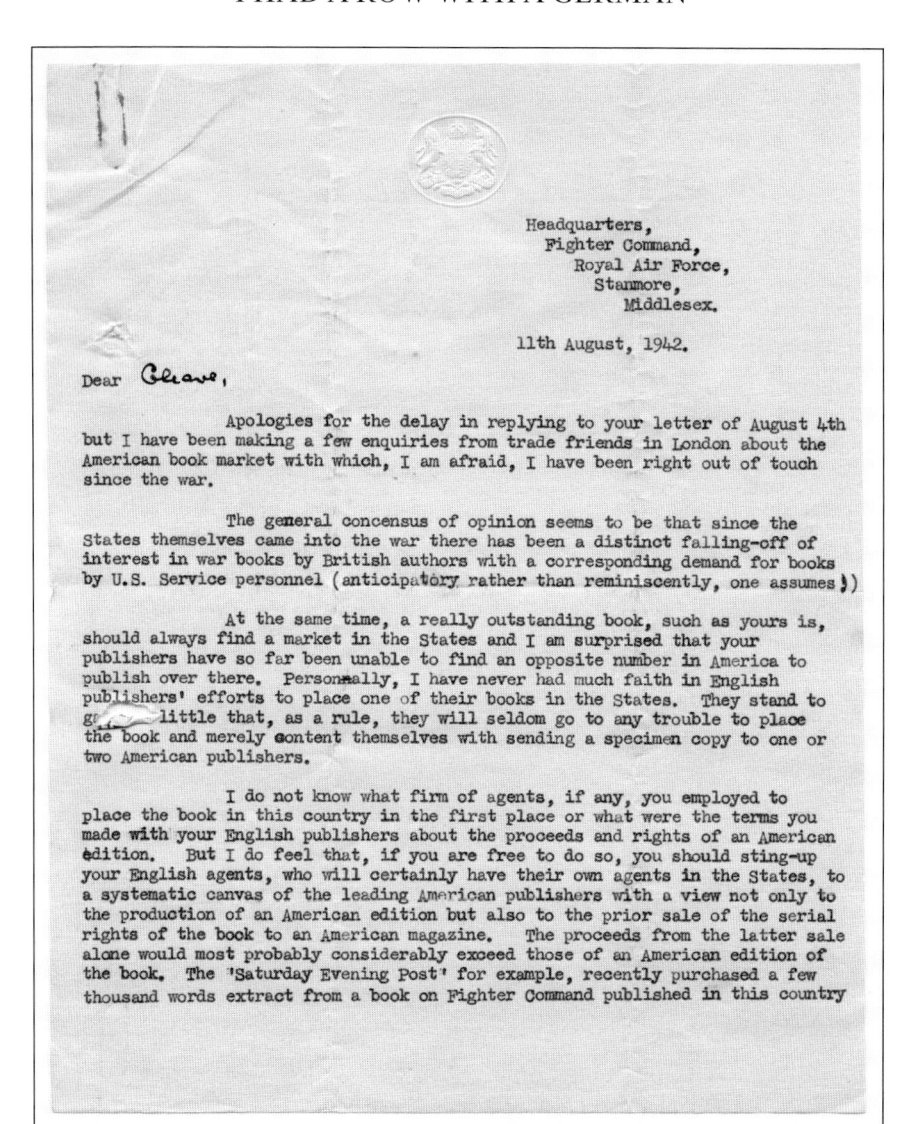

> Headquarters,
> Fighter Command,
> Royal Air Force,
> Stanmore,
> Middlesex.
>
> 11th August, 1942.
>
> Dear Cleave,
>
> Apologies for the delay in replying to your letter of August 4th but I have been making a few enquiries from trade friends in London about the American book market with which, I am afraid, I have been right out of touch since the war.
>
> The general concensus of opinion seems to be that since the States themselves came into the war there has been a distinct falling-off of interest in war books by British authors with a corresponding demand for books by U.S. Service personnel (anticipatory rather than reminiscently, one assumes!)
>
> At the same time, a really outstanding book, such as yours is, should always find a market in the States and I am surprised that your publishers have so far been unable to find an opposite number in America to publish over there. Personally, I have never had much faith in English publishers' efforts to place one of their books in the States. They stand to gain so little that, as a rule, they will seldom go to any trouble to place the book and merely content themselves with sending a specimen copy to one or two American publishers.
>
> I do not know what firm of agents, if any, you employed to place the book in this country in the first place or what were the terms you made with your English publishers about the proceeds and rights of an American edition. But I do feel that, if you are free to do so, you should sting-up your English agents, who will certainly have their own agents in the States, to a systematic canvas of the leading American publishers with a view not only to the production of an American edition but also to the prior sale of the serial rights of the book to an American magazine. The proceeds from the latter sale alone would most probably considerably exceed those of an American edition of the book. The 'Saturday Evening Post' for example, recently purchased a few thousand words extract from a book on Fighter Command published in this country

This letter from Headquarters Fighter Command, sent to Tom just a week before the Dieppe Raid, suggests that there had been some discussion concerning American sales for the book.

AFTER PUBLICATION

- 2 -

a few weeks ago and paid considerably over £150 for the extract alone.

The two American syndicates you mentioned might well be interested in acquiring serial rights (neither, so far as I know, has any book-publishing affiliations,) Mr. H. J. J. Sargent is the headman over here of North American Newspaper Alliance and their address is 30, Bouverie Street, London, E.C.4. Newspaper Enterprise Association is managed in London by Paul Manning (address: 72, Fleet Street, E.C.4) and both firms are quite likely purchasers of the American serial rights.

Finally, if you have not already got an English agent I would most strongly advise you to link up with one as soon as possible, preferably one with a good American organisation of its own or good contacts in the States. One I can recommend personally is Curtis, Brown Ltd., of 6 Henrietta Street, W.C.2. who have their own New York offices and who would competently handle both the serial and book rights for you in the States.

I hope you will find something slightly helpful in this rather long and rambling letter and if there is any point on which you would like me to be more specific, or any other way in which I can help at all, please let me know and I shall be only too glad to co-operate.

I keep promising myself the early pleasure of meeting you and am now going to make a really determined effort to get down to Manston before your next book (which I hope is already on the stocks) is launched!

Yours sincerely,

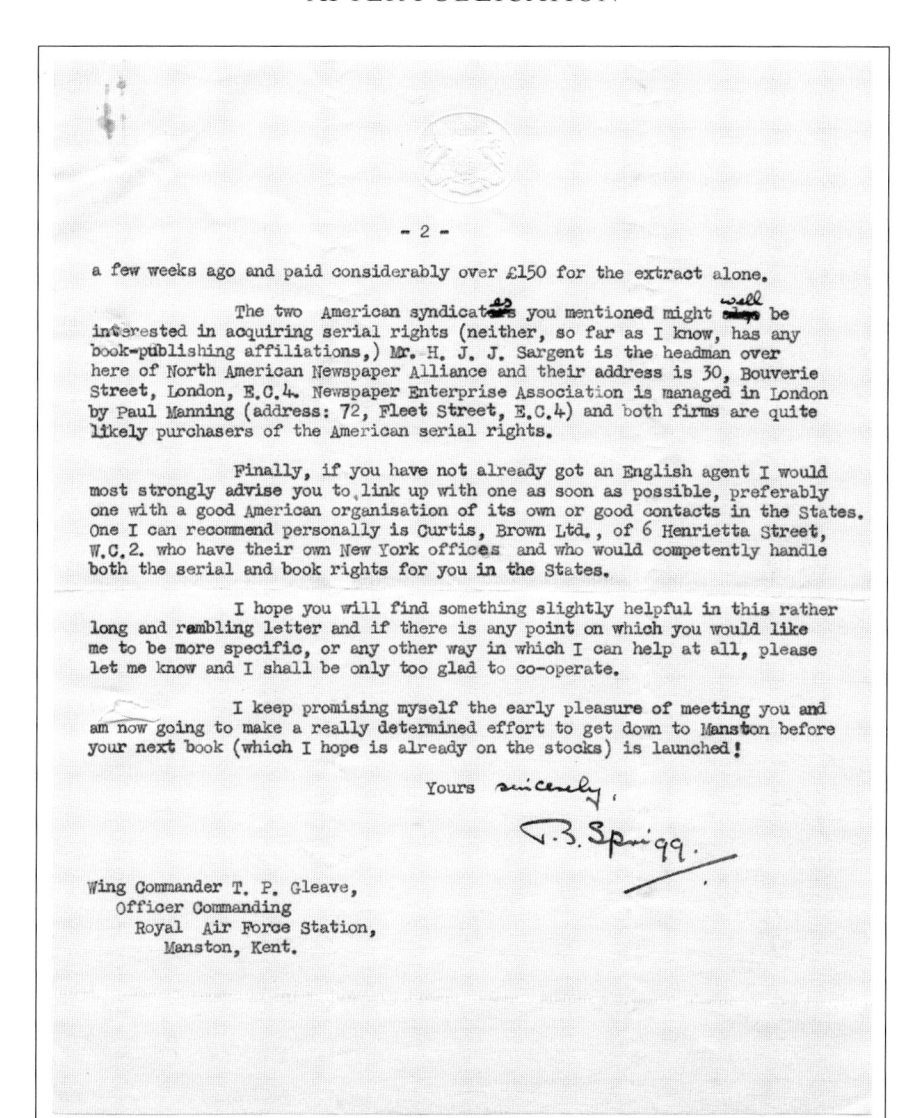

T. B. Sprigg.

Wing Commander T. P. Gleave,
   Officer Commanding
      Royal Air Force Station,
         Manston, Kent.

The second page of the letter from Headquarters Fighter Command dated 11 August 1942.

I HAD A ROW WITH A GERMAN

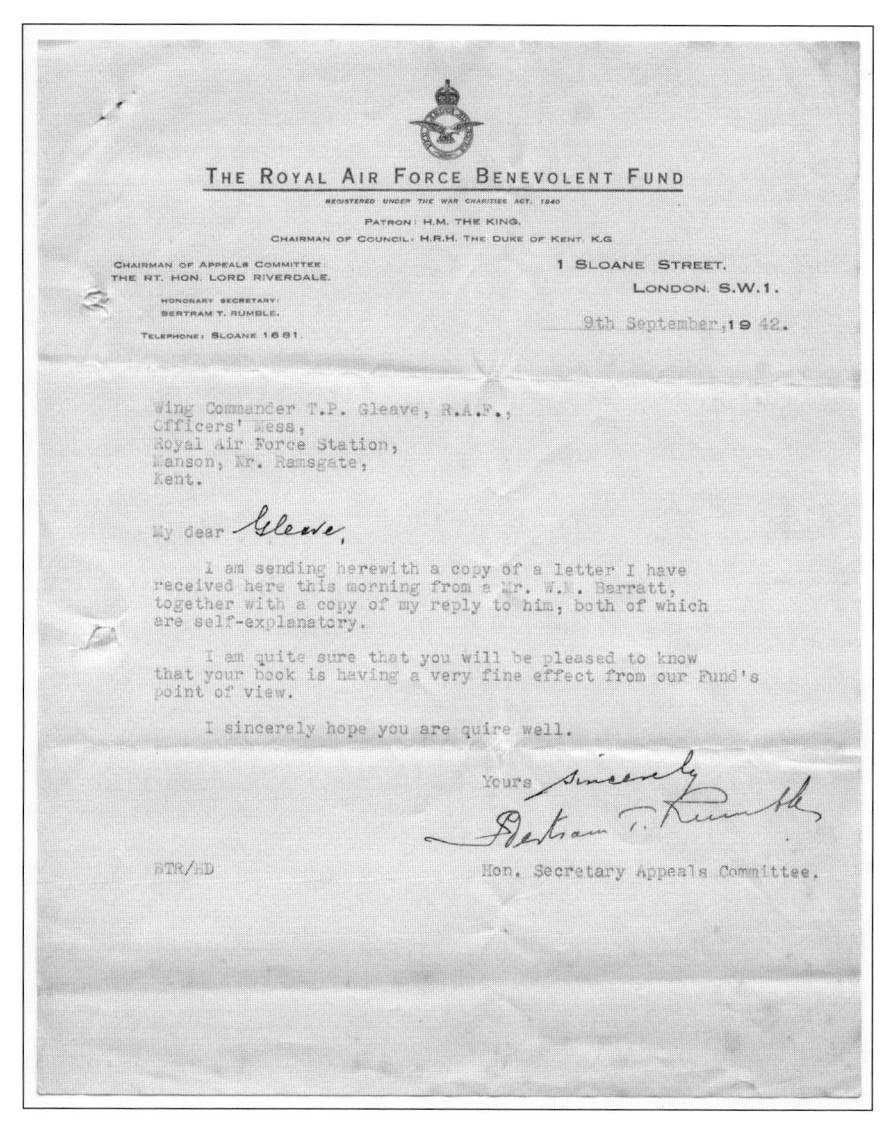

> **THE ROYAL AIR FORCE BENEVOLENT FUND**
> REGISTERED UNDER THE WAR CHARITIES ACT, 1940
> PATRON: H.M. THE KING.
> CHAIRMAN OF COUNCIL: H.R.H. THE DUKE OF KENT, K.G
>
> CHAIRMAN OF APPEALS COMMITTEE:
> THE RT. HON. LORD RIVERDALE.
> HONORARY SECRETARY:
> BERTRAM T. RUMBLE.
> TELEPHONE: SLOANE 1681.
>
> 1 SLOANE STREET,
> LONDON. S.W.1.
>
> 9th September, 1942.
>
> Wing Commander T.P. Gleave, R.A.F.,
> Officers' Mess,
> Royal Air Force Station,
> Manson, Nr. Ramsgate,
> Kent.
>
> My dear Gleave,
>
> I am sending herewith a copy of a letter I have received here this morning from a Mr. W.M. Barratt, together with a copy of my reply to him, both of which are self-explanatory.
>
> I am quite sure that you will be pleased to know that your book is having a very fine effect from our Fund's point of view.
>
> I sincerely hope you are quite well.
>
> Yours sincerely,
> Bertram T. Rumble
>
> BTR/HD
> Hon. Secretary Appeals Committee.

The publication of *I Had a Row With a German* had the effect that Tom, his publishers and the RAF Benevolent Fund had hoped for – as this letter from the latter on 9 September 1942 suggests.

AFTER PUBLICATION

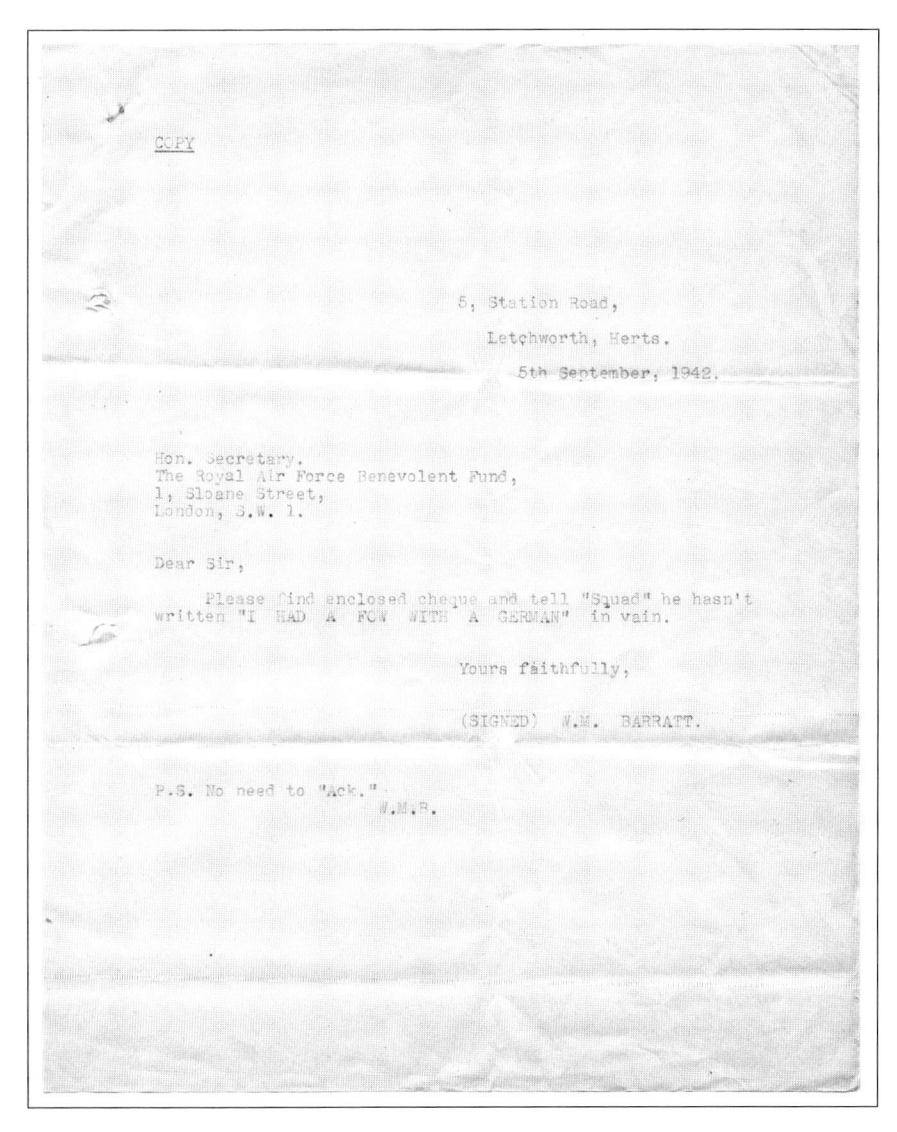

> COPY
>
> 5, Station Road,
> Letchworth, Herts.
> 5th September, 1942.
>
> Hon. Secretary,
> The Royal Air Force Benevolent Fund,
> 1, Sloane Street,
> London, S.W. 1.
>
> Dear Sir,
>
> Please find enclosed cheque and tell "Squad" he hasn't written "I HAD A FOW WITH A GERMAN" in vain.
>
> Yours faithfully,
>
> (SIGNED) W.M. BARRATT.
>
> P.S. No need to "Ack."
> W.M.B.

The communication from W.M. Barratt that, dated 5 September 1942, was sent to Tom by Bertram T. Rumble on 9 September.

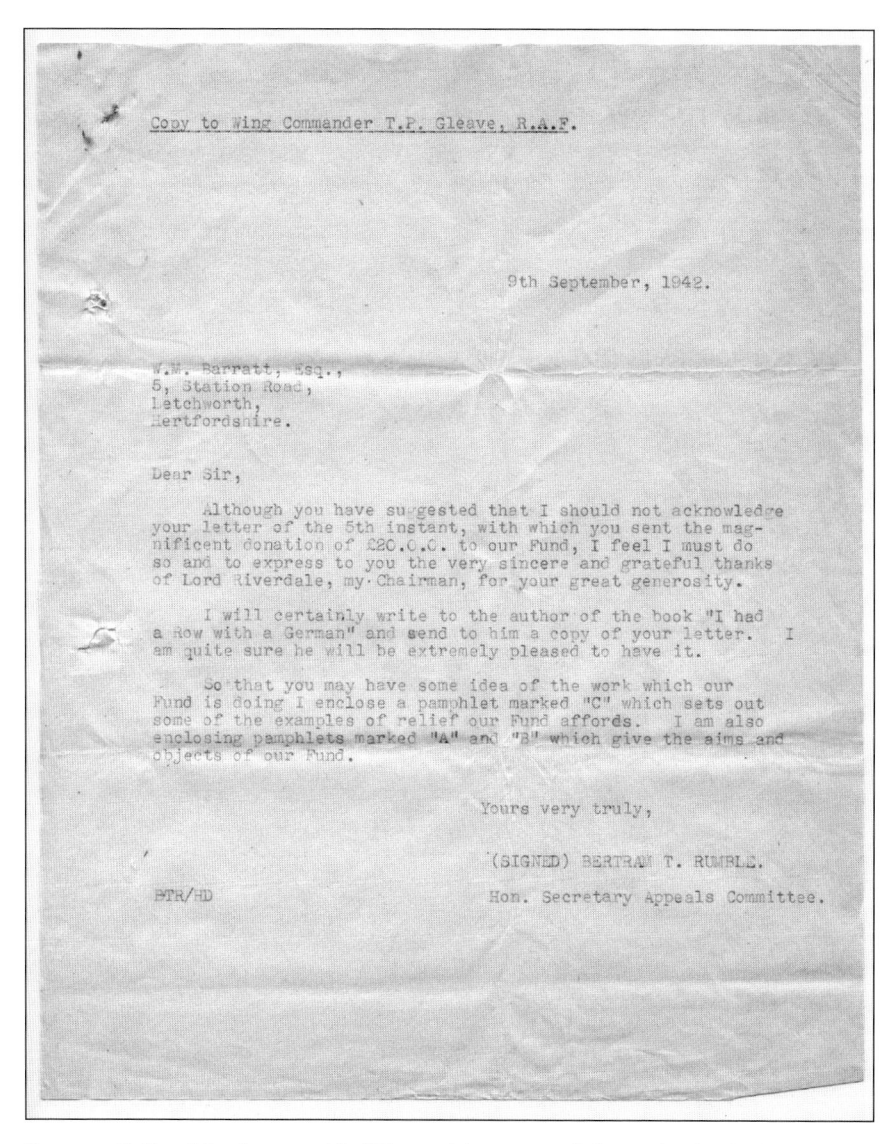

> Copy to Wing Commander T.P. Gleave, R.A.F.
>
> 9th September, 1942.
>
> W.M. Barratt, Esq.,
> 5, Station Road,
> Letchworth,
> Hertfordshire.
>
> Dear Sir,
>
> Although you have suggested that I should not acknowledge your letter of the 5th instant, with which you sent the magnificent donation of £20.0.0. to our Fund, I feel I must do so and to express to you the very sincere and grateful thanks of Lord Riverdale, my Chairman, for your great generosity.
>
> I will certainly write to the author of the book "I had a Row with a German" and send to him a copy of your letter. I am quite sure he will be extremely pleased to have it.
>
> So that you may have some idea of the work which our Fund is doing I enclose a pamphlet marked "C" which sets out some of the examples of relief our Fund affords. I am also enclosing pamphlets marked "A" and "B" which give the aims and objects of our Fund.
>
> Yours very truly,
>
> (SIGNED) BERTRAM T. RUMBLE.
> Hon. Secretary Appeals Committee.
>
> BTR/HD

Bertram T. Rumble also provided Tom with a copy of the reply that he had sent to W.M. Barratt regarding his donation inspired by the book.

AFTER PUBLICATION

The Royal Air Force Benevolent Fund.
PATRON: H.M. THE KING.
CHAIRMAN: H.R.H. THE DUKE OF KENT, K.G.

Telephone No.: HOVE 3992.
All Communications to be addressed to the Secretary

EATON HOUSE,
14, EATON ROAD,
HOVE, SUSSEX.

Our Reference IB. U. 1630.

27th November, 1942.

Group Captain. T.P. Gleave.
2. Mowbray Road.
Brondesbury.
London. N. W. 6.

Dear Sir,

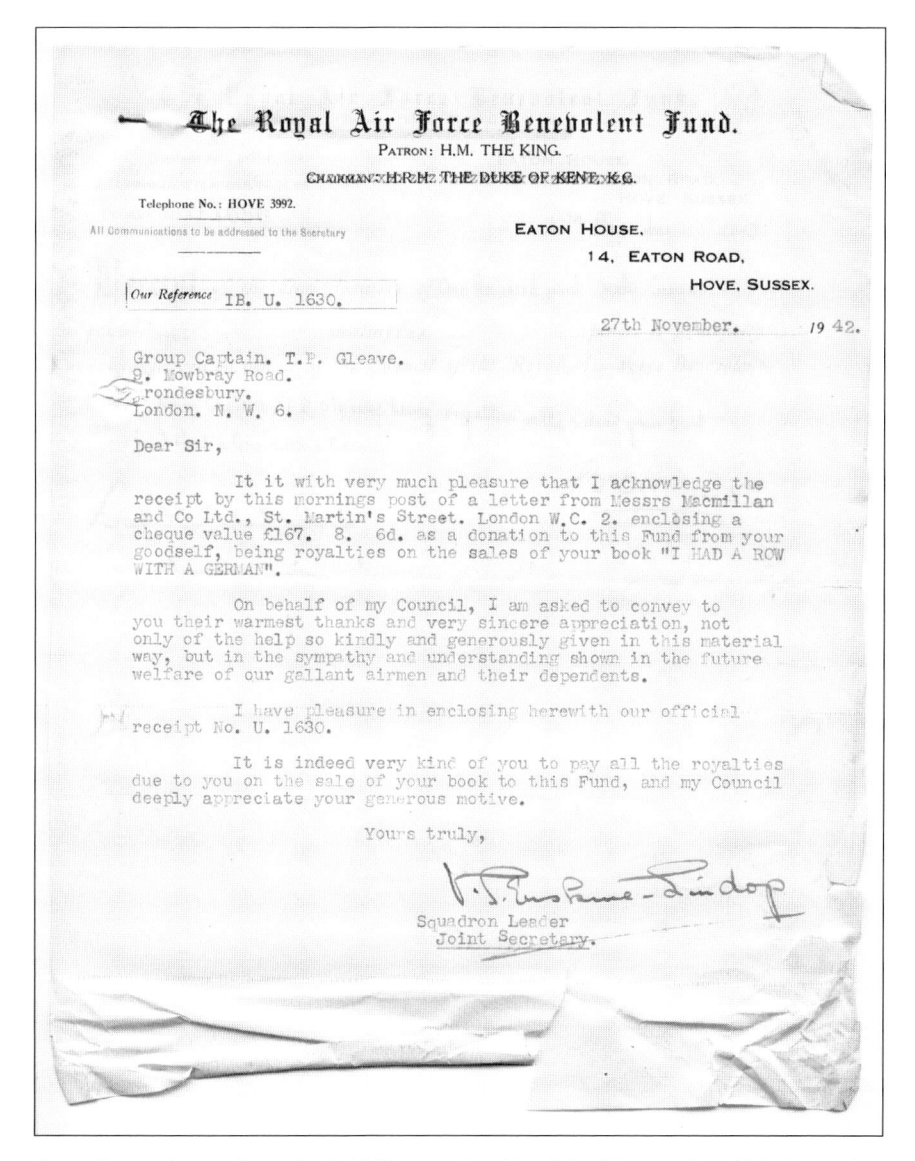

It it with very much pleasure that I acknowledge the receipt by this mornings post of a letter from Messrs Macmillan and Co Ltd., St. Martin's Street. London W.C. 2. enclosing a cheque value £167. 8. 6d. as a donation to this Fund from your goodself, being royalties on the sales of your book "I HAD A ROW WITH A GERMAN".

On behalf of my Council, I am asked to convey to you their warmest thanks and very sincere appreciation, not only of the help so kindly and generously given in this material way, but in the sympathy and understanding shown in the future welfare of our gallant airmen and their dependents.

I have pleasure in enclosing herewith our official receipt No. U. 1630.

It is indeed very kind of you to pay all the royalties due to you on the sale of your book to this Fund, and my Council deeply appreciate your generous motive.

Yours truly,

[signature]
Squadron Leader
Joint Secretary.

One of many letters from the RAF Benevolent Fund, in this case dated 27 November 1942, which informed Tom of the receipt of funds from the sales of his book.

I HAD A ROW WITH A GERMAN

> Netherturn
> St Andrews
> Fife
>
> Nov 14. 1943
>
> Messrs Macmillan & Co.
> Publishers.
>
> Dear Sirs, I am very anxious to get in touch with the author of "I had a Row with a German," whose book was published by your firm under the pseudonym of "R.A.F. Casualty". My reason is that he writes of my son in this book - and describes his death in the Battle of Britain on August 30. 1940. My son is called Jenks in the book - but his real name was Pilot-Officer David Nicholas Owen Jenkins, and all the facts in the book fit in with my son's brief career in the R.A.F. he was only just 21 when he was killed. If you could forward this letter to the above author, I should be very grateful. Yours faithfully
> (Mrs) Horatia M. Jenkins

Among the extensive correspondence that Tom Gleave kept in his files are three letters from Horatia Mary Jenkins – the first one being seen here. Mrs Jenkins was, as she points out, the mother of Pilot Officer David Nicholas Owen Jenkins, a fellow 253 Squadron pilot who is mentioned in Tom's book, in which he is referred to as 'Jenks'.

> Netherburn
> St. Andrews
> Fife.
>
> Dec. 12 1943.
>
> Dear Group-Captain Gleave
>
> Thank you very much for so kindly writing to me about your book, and the mention of my son Nicholas in it. One clings to the smallest item of any record of those who are gone, and whose going has left life so empty for us here – I had a nice letter from F/O Pring, who was Adjutant to 253 then, but that was all, as of course the Battle of Britain was in full progress, and the squadron was suffering such heavy losses. I feel happy to think that you thought well of Nicholas, (as he certainly appreciated you) and that he seems to have been good & competent at his job. After his death, I received

The first page of the second letter Mrs Jenkins' sent to Tom Gleave. Her son was shot down in combat over Redhill on 30 August 1940. He baled out but did not survive.

> more than 300 letters about him, some from complete strangers to me — and mentioning qualities in him which we had never appreciated. At home he was just loved. He was always "fey" about flying, & I think had some special instinct for it, as he seems to have done very well. — I am glad to think that his courage did not fail "even unto the death." He is buried in Cotswold, in a tiny village where he was born, and next to his father, who died when Nick was only nine weeks old —
>
> We also knew some of the other people mentioned by you. Wally Nowak the Pole, Roy Watts the "Walrus" flyer, & one or two others, "Curly" Clifton, who was a friend of his; some of them he brought over when they were at Turnhouse.
>
> He was absolutely miserable when they were moved to Prestwick on Aug 21

The second page of Mrs Jenkins' second letter. Pilot Officer Jenkins' Hurricane, P3921, fell to earth at Butlers Dene Road in Woldingham, Surrey. The son of the Revd. Canon William Owen Jenkins, D.D. and Horatia Mary Jenkins, of St. Andrews, Fife, he was buried in Bagendon (St. Margaret) Churchyard in Gloucestershire.

AFTER PUBLICATION

> 2
> as he felt it was a backwater, & that they would be left out of the fighting. Actually he was allowed a 'Magister' on the 27, & came home for two days leave, so was here when the order came at 2.a.m on 29, to go back to Prestwick at dawn – He flew over this house at about 8.30. from Lenchars, & that was the last we saw of him. Though he rang up my daughter from Prestwick to tell us he was going "south" to where his car was". F/O Pring rang up on Friday night to say he was gone. so it all seemed terribly sudden to us –
> I am perfectly certain on looking back at that morning that he knew he would never come home again –
> The only comfort left is the equal certainty that he is still

In her second letter, of which this is the third page, Mrs Jenkins notes how in the aftermath of her son's death she received more than 300 letters – many from complete strangers to her.

I HAD A ROW WITH A GERMAN

> *helping in this awful war —*
>
> *May I thank you for your delightful book, beautifully written and full of interest quite apart from our personal one. It is odd that I first heard of it from a stepdaughter of mine out in South Africa! The whole subject is tremendously interesting, and the progress & patience of your restoration a wonderful record.*
>
> *I am glad that Nick was killed instantly, & not shot while coming down in his parachute like Cpn. L. Starr. His watch (broken) pointed to 12 o'clock, & his ring which I have on, was also broken in half.—*
>
> *Thankyou again for your letter. Nick was lucky to be commanded by you.*
>
> *Yours sincerely*
> *Horatia M. Jenkins*

The last page of Mrs Jenkins' second letter to Tom Gleave. In some of her last words, she wrote: 'I am so glad that Nick was killed instantly, and not shot while coming down in his parachute.'

AFTER PUBLICATION

> Netherburn
> 15. 1. 44.   St Andrews. Fife.
>
> Dear Group-Captain Gleave,
>
> Thank you very much indeed for sending me a copy of your book. I feel very proud of it "from the author," & shall treasure it greatly. Several people to whom I gave copies of the book are co tremendously interested in the wonderful account of your patient bearing of illness and your cure.
>
> I hope that the exigencies of war (or peace) may someday cross our paths. Perhaps you can bring your family to St Andrews for a holiday, it is a good spot in the summer & autumn.
>
> With kind regards
> Yours very sincerely &
> gratefully
> Horatia M. Jenkins

The last of Mrs Jenkins' letters that Tom Gleave retained in his files.

I HAD A ROW WITH A GERMAN

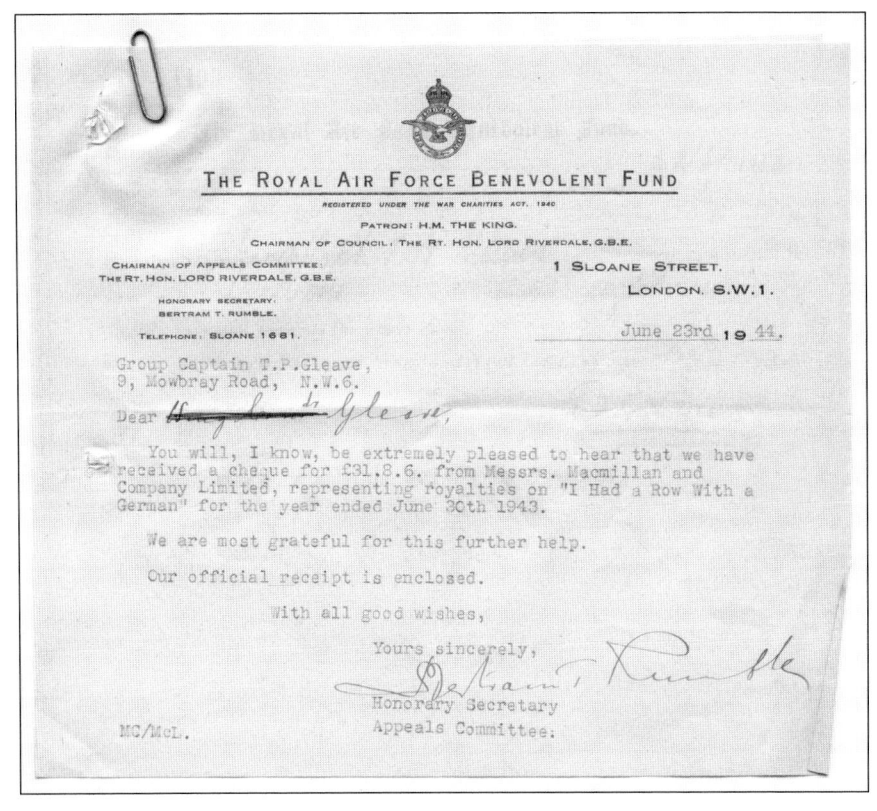

The sales of *I Had a Row With a German* continued to generate numerous donations to the RAF Benevolent Fund, as this correspondence dated 23 June 1944, relating to monies received from Macmillan & Co., testifies.

AFTER PUBLICATION

> **THE ROYAL AIR FORCE BENEVOLENT FUND**
> REGISTERED UNDER THE WAR CHARITIES ACT. 1940.
> PATRON: H.M. THE KING.
> PRESIDENT: H.R.H. THE DUCHESS OF KENT.
> CHAIRMAN OF COUNCIL: THE RT. HON. LORD RIVERDALE, G.B.E.
>
> CHAIRMAN OF APPEALS COMMITTEE:
> THE RT. HON. LORD RIVERDALE, G.B.E.
> HON. SECRETARY: BERTRAM T. RUMBLE.
> TELEPHONE: SLOANE 1681.
>
> 1 SLOANE STREET,
> LONDON. S.W.1.
>
> October 19th, 1944.
>
> Group Captain Gleave,
> 9, Mowbray Road,
> Brondesbury, N.W.6.
>
> Dear Group Captain Gleave,
>
> I know you will be delighted to hear that we have received a donation of £40.10.6. from Messrs. Macmillan & Company Limited, as a result of sales of your book "I Had A Row With A German".
>
> I do not have to tell you how grateful we are to you for this further support, and particularly so at this time when the Royal Air Force figures so prominently in the daily news.
>
> Yours sincerely,
>
> Bertram T. Rumble
> Honorary Secretary
> Appeals Committee.
>
> MC/McL.   *I hope you are well.*

Another letter from the RAF Benevolent Fund, this time dated 19 October 1944, informed Tom that a further sum had been received from Macmillan & Co.

APPENDICES

Appendix I

Tom Gleave's Combat Reports

Date	**30/8/40**
Flight, Squadron:	'B' Flight, 253
Number of Enemy Aircraft:	13
Type of Enemy Aircraft:	Me 109
Time Attack Was Delivered:	Approx. 1720
Place Attack Was Delivered:	Near Dungeness
Height of Enemy:	17,000 (Dived from Sun)
Enemy Casualties:	One Me 109 Destroyed
Our Casualties, Aircraft:	Nil
Personnel:	Nil
Searchlights:	N/A
Anti-Aircraft guns:	No
Range at which fire was opened:	180-200 yds, closing to less than 70 yds. One continuous 12 sec. burst

General Report

I was Leader of "B" Flight – Blue and Green Sections – three and four a/c respectively. At approx. 1700 hrs. we were ordered to patrol base at 1500ft. order received just after take-off to proceed S.E. and climb to 15,000ft. A few miles S.E. of Tunbridge Wells, Green Section turned East; the leader rocking a/c and informing me of E/A to the East of us. They proved to be Hurricanes and Green Section turned South.

I HAD A ROW WITH A GERMAN

I also turned and opened up to regain position and shortly afterwards tracer and cannon tracks appeared over Green Section. I turned Blue Section and sighted 7 Me 109's coming down from Sun with six more a short distance behind, all in line astern. Scrap developed into fast circling melee all firing ahead. Saw Me 109 on tail of Hurricane blowing off fabric and wood. Fastened onto E/A and give him along 12 second burst from 180-200 yds. range to less than 70 yds.

E/A continued to turn behind Hurricane for a few seconds, then rolled onto back, flew inverted for a while. I kept firing and saw patches of black material coming away from starboard wing near wing root and from fuselage. A piece of wire or metal dropped away as E/A turned, still inverted and dropped into dive. Forced to leave E/A as three 109's were fastened on my tail. Dived all out, turning and threw them off and climbed again returning to scene of fight.

No a/c to be seen nor [*illegible*] signs of damaged Hurricane. Returned to base. Damaged Hurricane safe on tarmac. E/A's destruction confirmed after landing.

***

TOM GLEAVE'S COMBAT REPORTS

Date	**30/8/40**
Flight, Squadron:	'A' Flight, 253, Emergency Section
Number of Enemy Aircraft:	Approximately 50 a/c
Type of Enemy Aircraft:	Me 109
Time Attack Was Delivered:	Approx. 1143 hrs.
Place Attack Was Delivered:	Three to four miles West of Maidstone
Height of Enemy:	17,500 ft
Enemy Casualties: Destroyed	Four Me 109s Probably
Our Casualties, Aircraft:	Zero
Personnel:	Zero
Searchlights:	N/A
Anti-Aircraft guns:	No
Range at which fire was opened:	(i) 175 yds. Four sec. burst
	(ii) 120 yds. Four sec. burst
	(iii) 60-70 yds. Five sec. burst
	(iv) 75 yds. Emptied guns

General Report

I was Leader of Emergency Section with F/Lt. Brown as No. 2 and P/O Francis as No. 3. At approx. 11.30 hrs. we were ordered off to patrol base at 2,000ft. at 1,700ft. we were ordered to climb to 20,000ft. in a South Easterly direction.

At 17,500ft. large formation of 109's sighted travelling S.S.E. Attacked from sun into E.A.'s flank. Attacked one Me 109 at angle of 20 deg. to line of flight – 175 yds. range – with four sec. burst. Shot appeared to enter fuselage near cockpit and engine cowling. Tracer appeared to spiral fuselage and come aft, believe this was shattered Perspex. E.A

I HAD A ROW WITH A GERMAN

turned on back and dived vertically down. Tracer and cannon passed each side of me and I dipped turning right and left and pulled up.

No sign of No. 2 or No. 3. E/A crossed my sights at 120 yds. range. Gave him 4 sec. burst. Column of black smoke burst from what appeared to be leading edge of starboard plane, about 3ft, from wing root. E/A turned across my path and dropped into dive leaving long column of black smoke in his wake.

Pulled up to avoid collision with this E/A and nearly collided with another 109 who flew straight across my sight at 60-70yds. range. Gave him 3 sec. burst. E/A pulled the nose up, appeared to lose speed rapidly and fall out of sky as though stalling into a dive. Gave him another short two-sec. burst to help him on.

Cockpit appeared empty but saw no body leave a/c. turned towards sun to evade tracer and cannon. An Me 109 passed just to the right and slightly above and ahead. Gave him all I had at about 75 yds. range. Shot appeared to go slap into under-part of cockpit and fuselage. E/A rolled on back, flew inverted for a few seconds and then went into vertical dive still going all out. Dived from scrap to throw off 109's on my tail.

No sign of No. 2 or No. 3. Both missing. Returned to aerodrome.

***

TOM GLEAVE'S COMBAT REPORTS

Date   31/8/40

Flight, Squadron: 'A' & 'B' Flight, 253
Number of Enemy Aircraft: Large formation covering large area
Type of Enemy Aircraft: Ju 88s
Time Attack Was Delivered: Approx. 1245 hrs.
Place Attack Was Delivered: Near Orpington
Height of Enemy: Approx. 12,000-15,000 ft
Enemy Casualties: 1 Ju 88 Destroyed
Our Casualties,   Aircraft: One
                  Personnel: One
Searchlights: N/A
Anti-Aircraft guns: No
Range at which fire was opened: (i) 200 to 100 yds.   5 to 6 sec. burst
                                   (ii) 200 to 100 yds. 5 to 6 sec. burst

General Report

I was Leader of 253 Sqdn. composed of 7 a/c. At 1238 hrs. we were ordered to take-off and climb to 2,000ft. to join up with Squadron from Croydon.

At 1,000ft. sighted other Squadron coming South in an inverted 'J' formation. Joined up to form inverted 'U' formation. Formation turned over base and at a height of 12-15,000ft. I glanced up and sighted extensive formation of Ju 88's flying in several parallel lines of a/c line astern. They were 1,000ft. above and closing distance rapidly.

When within M.G. range own formation still forged ahead and I decided to attack before E/A opened fire. Pulled up and fired raking burst at No.5 of line of Ju 88's immediately above. Faked stall turn at top of climb and dived, repeating process on No. 3 of E./A. As I turned

I HAD A ROW WITH A GERMAN

over at top of climb I saw clouds of greyish white smoke pouring from port engine of No. 3 of E/A. Received incendiary in starboard tank as I dived to attack No. 1 of E/A.

Own a/c burst into flames. Attempted to localise or put-out fire by rocking and skidding at the same time losing speed. Fire increased, tried to get out but unable to move owing to burns, a/c blew up and I was blown clear.

Descended by parachute and taken to hospital at Orpington.

Note: In his own notes, Tom wrote: 'Official score: one confirmed and four probable. Researchers have found five confirmed on 30th August (all Me.109's) and one Ju.88 confirmed on 31st August (crashed at Provins in France), making a total bag of six. A 'possible' crashed at Chateaudun.'

Appendix II

Selected Wartime Reviews

R.A.F. AUTHORS

We shall have to wait until after the war for most of the "classic" stories of the exploits of the R.A.F. Conditions of active service do not permit the author-aviator the necessary leisure to write a "full length" and considered book.

But already many short studies of the R.A.F. have appeared in print, and some of them are remarkably well written. There seems no dearth of literary talent in the service.

Out of a batch of R.A.F. publications which have recently arrived in this office, we select a little book entitled *I Had a Row with a German* for brief comment. The author simply signs himself "R.A.F. Casualty." He was one of the brilliant young pilots who took part in the Battle of Britain when it was at its fiercest.

I Had a Row with a German is not remarkable for its literary competence. It is written simply, modestly, and earnestly. The author was wounded badly – his skin was almost entirely burnt off. He writes his book while convalescing, while waiting to return to his flying duties. It seems to reflect admirably the faith of a thoughtful, intelligent, courageous pilot to whom the glamour and adventure of flying are secondary to the ideal for which we are fighting. His gratitude to those who have nursed him back to health preoccupies him far more than the thrilling combats in which he has taken part. The entire royalties of the book are to go to the R.A.F. Benevolent Fund.

The Scotsman, 15 January 1942

***

SELECTED WARTIME REVIEWS

BOOKS OF THE DAY

By Charles E. Byles

While recording the Army's exploits, Major Yeats-Brown pays incidental tribute to the sister Services. Recalling the beauty of that 1940 autumn, when in the Battle of Britain the many were saved by the few, he writes: "As if to lighten the hearts of those who served her, England whispered to them: 'Am I not fair, and worthy of sacrifice?' Young men went forth to their glorious deeds – and to their death – in the skies above her, and soldiers, sailors, workers served her as Helen was served when the world was young, and Troy beleaguered."

The comparison is not altogether fanciful, for I have just come across a passage in a fighter-pilot's reminiscences which reveals a feeling for the home landscape almost in the heat of action. This description of the "smiling garden of England," seen from a point 17,000 ft. above Maidstone, just before an encounter with the enemy, occurs in a vivid, though unpretentious, little book called *I Had a Row with a German*." By "R.A.F. Casualty." With 8 Illustrations (Macmillan; 5s.).

The author tells his tale with straightforward simplicity. He had vowed to "rid the earth of one German, even if it cost me my neck." The chance came when he was made a squadron-leader ("Squad" to his friends), and before his own crash he disposed of a good many more. Blown out of a blazing 'plane, he was saved by his parachute, but seriously burned, and the story ends in a hospital specialising in facial reconstruction by plastic surgery.

Nothing could convey better than this book the wonderful spirit of our airmen, their zeal to be up and doing, their absolute love of danger, their joyous comradeship, and their fierce hatred of an unchivalrous foe who would shoot a defenceless man descending by parachute.

Illustrated London News, 24 January 1942

***

I HAD A ROW WITH A GERMAN

FIGHTER PILOT'S STORY

In *I Had a Row with a German* (Macmillan & Co., Ltd., 5s. net), one of the matchless few whose heroism was given tribute in Mr. Churchill's memorable sentence in Parliament, tells in simple, straightforward manner a story of gallantry which cannot fail to rouse the reader's interest.

"R.A.F. Casualty," he prefers to call himself, has no need to embroider his tale with fanciful language in order to make it a vivid, dramatic narrative. The plain, unvarnished account of his experiences from the outbreak of war to the moment in the Battle of Britain when he crashed in flames is gripping enough.

In this little book a brave, unassuming fighter pilot, who fought and was badly wounded, speaks not only for himself, but also for those thousands of others who serve the cause of freedom in the R.A.F. The volume is illustrated with admirable photographs, and the author has arranged for all royalties from the sales of the book to be given to the R.A.P. Benevolent Fund.

Burnley Express, 4 April 1942

***

SELECTED WARTIME REVIEWS

BY "ONE OF THE FEW"

An Airman Tells His Story
THEN PUTS A QUESTION

The heroism of the Royal Air Force as a body evokes homage from all. But the measure of our debt cannot be appreciated in the least bit until we remember that it is due to instances of great fortitude, intrepid courage and high spirit in one individual, multiplied a thousand fold.

Herein lies the absorbing appeal of *I Had a Row with a German* (Macmillan and Co., Ltd., 5s.), written by a "R.A.F. Casualty." It is just a straightforward narrative of the Service life of just one airman who became a wing commander; there are no frills, no attempt at glamour, no purple patches.

The story is objective even when it tells how the writer was sent to earth in what must have been a mass of flames. Still more striking is the insight he gives into the marvels of skin grafting, by which the scars of many terrible burns are almost obliterated. And the writer has every right to conclude, concerning his colleagues who also survive, though maimed and crippled: "They remain, and we are their trustees. We owe them no less a debt. Must they, like many of their counterparts of a generation ago, know poverty and feel the soul-stirring torment of grudging charity? Must they be victims of life's most vicious crime – man's ingratitude to man? … To say 'You have done your bit' means little to one to whom a monotonous existence brings torture of the soul far greater than torture of the body. May we, in the aftermath of 'this our finest hour,' keep our sacred trust!"

Read that again after you have read the preceding story of one air hero's career, and remember that all the royalties from the sale of the book go to the R.A.F. Benevolent Fund.

Norwood News, 30 January 1942

***

I HAD A ROW WITH A GERMAN

DAY TO DAY IN LIVERPOOL
By The Post Man

It is an open secret that "R.A.F. Casualty," author of *I Had a Row with a German* (Macmillan, 5s), is Wing-Commander T. Percy Gleave. of Blundellsands, where he lived with his parents in Dowhills Road until his marriage two or three years before the war.

The frontispiece-portrait, illustrating the marvels of facial surgery, is not so altered as a sensitive victim imagines, and this, coupled with the word-picture of Liverpool Bay as seen from Blundellsands shore, immediately established his identity to a large circle of friends and acquaintances.

Wing-Commander Gleave's exciting and cheery book, all profits from which go to the R.A.F. Benevolent Fund, deals with the experiences of a squadron-leader in the Battle of Britain who baled out after a flight over Kent, badly burned, and with his long and painful convalescence, cheerfully borne, in many hospitals, resulting in almost complete recovery.

Promoted from squadron-leader to wing commander last year, the author has resumed full service, has again flown on many occasions, and is at present in command of an aerodrome in the South of England.

Liverpool Daily Post, 17 February 1942

***

SELECTED WARTIME REVIEWS

FIGHTER-PILOT

I Had a Row with a German, by "R.A.F. Casualty," (Macmillan 5/-). The author, a pilot in a fighter squadron, took part in the aerial battles over Britain in the summer of 1940. After several successful encounters his 'plane was set on fire and he was blown out of the cockpit, landing by parachute, badly burned.

This is the story of his life in the R.A.F., of battles in the skies by night and day, of comrades who fought and won or crashed and died, of terrible sufferings pluckily borne. It is told by a soldier in a soldier's blunt fashion and provides an interesting picture of a fighter-pilot's life.

Irish Independent, 9 February 1942

***

I HAD A ROW WITH A GERMAN

FIGHTER PILOT'S ADVENTURES

"A Modest Story of Gallantry and Fortitude"

Air Vice-Marshal T. Leigh-Mallory, who has written a short foreword to *I Had a Row with a German*, rightly describes it as "a modest story of gallantry and fortitude."

The author, who disguises his identity under the pen-name, "R.A.F. Casualty," is a fighter pilot who fought and was badly burned in the Battle of Britain. When war broke out, he had been ten years in the Air Service – part of it in Northern Ireland – and his duties lay at Fighter Command Headquarters; but he wanted to fly again, and at last was attached to a Hurricane squadron, and eventually took command of it.

Stationed in Eastern England, he spent long hours looking for Germans to shoot, and his narrative makes clear some of the great difficulties the night fighter must overcome.

The writer has given very vivid accounts of aerial dog fights in the Battle of Britain. In one he shot down four enemy machines, and was credited with two "probables" and two "possibles." In another he bagged one enemy machine.

Then, in some detail, he describes the fight in which his machine was set on fire, and relates how, terribly burned, he baled out and got to hospital. The third section of the book tells of the wonderful work that is being done in war hospitals, especially for those who have been burned. "A few more weeks and I shall be back on duty with a new face, strong limbs, and new life. A few more months and I shall be flying again." The book is published by Macmillan & Co. at 5s.

Belfast News-Letter, 13 February 1942

***

SELECTED WARTIME REVIEWS

AIR EDDIES
By Oliver Stewart

Air and hot air do not mix. Or, to put it plainly, flying a kite does not go well with shooting a line or telling the tale. The expert pilot, though, far from dumb, is often inarticulate. The result is that the full flame and fury of modern air war are rarely represented in the books. Yet there have been good first-hand accounts of air action, and I am going here to butt in on the book-of-the-month boys and proclaim my own choice.

I refer now to first-hand descriptive works alone, not to general discussions and reports of air matters, of which there have been many excellent examples. But of the first-hand accounts of air action, I can select only three: *Fighter Pilot*, *I Had a Row with a German*, and an astonishing fragment called *Dawn to Dusk*, which appears in the current issue of the *Royal Air Force Quarterly* …

I Had a Row with a German, is curious … it is written in conventional style … but it has three parts: one ordinary; one brilliantly descriptive and dealing with air fighting; and one soberly thoughtful and interesting dealing with the patching-up by a series of plastic operations of the author after he had baled out of his flaming aeroplane.

The Tatler, 14 January 1942

In Brief

I Had a Row With a German. By "R.A.F. Casualty." (Macmillan. 5s.)

The war so far has produced little of literature, but a great deal of what are known in the film trade as "documentaries." They are its best contribution to letters, simple, straightforward, unpretentious stories of jobs done and things seen. The most successful are those whose authors are strangers to the writing craft, and among the most successful should certainly rank this account of a pilot's joys, dangers, achievements, and defeat. In part it is little more than a war-diary, telling the day-to-day duties of a Fighter Squadron from September, 1939, until some day late in August, 1940, when the writer's machine was set ablaze 30,000 ft. above Kent, and he baled out, terribly burned, to face long months of hospital and eventual recovery with new eyelids, a new nose, but the old indomitable will and courage.

Not the least attractive feature of his book is the quite unconscious picture that it paints of genuine modesty and undramatised heroism.

A newspaper cutting from Tom Gleave's archives. Unfortunately, it is not known which publication this review was in.

SELECTED WARTIME REVIEWS

THE TIMES LITERARY SUPPLEMENT. 3 January 1942.

"I HAD A ROW WITH A GERMAN" By "R.A.F. Casualty." Macmillan 5s.

"What on earth have you been doing with yourself, darling?"
"Had a row with a German."

It was an embarrassing moment. The R.A.F. fighter pilot was in hospital, dreadfully burned after being shot down during the Battle of Britain, and these were the question and answer exchanged when his wife visited him for the first time – hence the title. For months the pilot lay between life and death. His face was disfigured, and new eyelids and a new nose were grafted. He received the modern salt bath treatment which has produced such wonderful results, and new skin was "cultivated" on various parts of his body. It must have been a dreary and painful experience, yet throughout the book there is not a single word of complaint. On the contrary, the pilot is almost pathetically grateful to all those who helped him – the man who carried him on his back to a farmhouse after he had made a parachute descent from his blazing Hurricane, the nurses who stayed with him during heavy air-raids, the doctors and orderlies, and fellow-patients who lit cigarettes for him while he was too helpless to do so for himself.

The book is well worth reading if only because it shows the qualities of modesty and courage which seem to be inherent in R.A.F. men. The book was written while the pilot was convalescing from injuries which had seemed likely to prove fatal, but already he was looking forward to the time when he would be back in the air having another "crack at the Hun"... "A few more weeks and I shall be back on duty with a new face, strong limbs and new life. A few more months and I shall be flying again." Instead of feeling that fate was unkind to single him out for such disfigurement his thoughts are all for those not so fortunate as himself, those who are maimed and crippled for life. He makes a touching appeal that they should not be victims of "life's most vicious crime – man's ingratitude to man," and, practising what he preaches, is devoting the royalties from his book to the R.A.F. Benevolent Fund.

A typed copy of the review of the book that appeared in *The Times* Literary Supplement on 3 January 1942.

Appendix III

Notes on Tom Gleave's Service Record

The following was compiled from a series of documents completed by Tom Gleave and which form part of his archives:

- Commissioned in the Royal Air Force as an Acting Pilot Officer in September 1930 and after three weeks at Uxbridge was posted to No.5 Flying Training School, Sealand, Cheshire. Passed out as an 'Exceptional' pilot in September 1931.
- Posted to No. 1 Fighter Squadron, Tangmere, as a Pilot Officer. Served with No. 1 Squadron until February 1934 during which time became a member of the Aerobatic Team, and passed 'Exceptional' as a Fighter Pilot. By this time had been promoted to Flying Officer.
- During February-May 1934, attended a Flying Instructor's Course at the Central Flying School. Passed out with Category "B2" and also qualified as an Instrument Flying Instructor.
- Posted in May 1934, to No. 5 Flying Training School at Sealand, Cheshire, as an Ab Initio and Fighter Flying Instructor. Lent to Oxford University Air Squadron (under Wing Commander Keith Park) 19 June to 3 August 1934.
- Member of the Sealand Aerobatic Team for British Empire Days. By then a Flight Lieutenant.
- At a demonstration at Catfoss on 22 September 1936, flying Audax K5241 solo, scored 94% hits on a towed flag. Believed to be a record which still stands.

NOTES ON TOM GLEAVE'S SERVICE RECORD

- Posted to No.502 (Ulster) Special Reserve Squadron as Squadron Flying Instructor, December 1936. Converted the Squadron to Auxiliary Status, becoming No. 502 (Ulster) Bomber Squadron, Auxiliary Air Force. Was re-posted as Adjutant and Chief Flying Instructor.
- Raised to Category "A1" as Flying Instructor on 17 July 1937.
- Promoted to Squadron Leader and posted to Headquarters Bomber Command as a Staff Officer in connection with Bomber Liaison duties at Fighter Command Operations Room, December 1938.
- During time at Bomber Command was also employed on writing Pilots' Notes and Maintenance Schedules for bomber aircraft, and drafting Air-Sea Rescue plans.
- Posted to Fighter Command on 3 September 1939, for full duties in the Operations Room as Bomber Liaison Officer (one of three). Main duty – identification of returning friendly bombers, until managing to get a squadron on 2 June 1940.
- Commanded No. 253 Squadron (Hurricanes) from 2 June to 9 August 1940, at Kirton-in-Lindsey and Turnhouse. Handed over Squadron to Squadron Leader Starr and allowed to stay with Squadron until called for by No.14 Group Commander. Starr killed a.m. 31 August. Took over command again. Self shot down at noon being blown out of Hurricane by explosion Landed by parachute near Biggin Hill and taken to Orpington Hospital.
- Promoted Wing Commander during stay at East Grinstead. Restored to non-operational flying in August 1941, flying in a Magister with Sgt. Anderson, also from No. 253 Squadron and a Guinea Pig. Made operationally fit, October 1941.
- Took temporary command of Royal Air Force, Northolt during illness of C.O., Group Captain McEvoy.
- Commanded R.A.F. Manston (neighbour of 'Hellfire Corner') 5 October 1941 to 12 April 1942.

- On 12 February 1942, put Operation *Fuller* into action to combat 'Channel Dash' of German battleships *Scharnhorst*, and *Gneisenau* and battlecruiser *Eugen*. Lost all six Swordfish of No. 825 Squadron, F.A.A. Only five survivors, three of whom were wounded. Put 'Winkle' Esmonde up for a V.C. which was awarded posthumously. Also put survivors up for awards, which all received. Hurricane fighter-bomber Squadron Leader put up for D.S.C. which he received. Others were decorated too. Losses among Hurricanes, Beauforts etc. aircraft were also tragic.
- Attended R.A.F. Staff College at Bulstrode Park, Gerrards Cross from 13 April to 9 July 1942.
- Commanded R.A.F. Manston again 10 July to 5 September 1942. Dieppe Raid was launched on 19 August 1942, and Manston became a main refuelling and re-arming base.
- Before leaving Manston on 6 September had pleaded for a long, wide concrete tarmac runway for saving Bomber Command and other Command aircraft damage on operations. Had photographs taken of wreckage after a particularly bad night for wreckage and sent them to Leigh-Mallory for onward transmission to Air Ministry. It did the trick, but took time to lay down runway. Today it is one of the emergency runways for civil and military aircraft, with FIDO fog disperser.
- Promoted Group Captain on 6 September 1942 and posted to the Special Planning Staff in Norfolk House (for Operation *Round Up* – later *Overlord*). Became the C.O.S.S.A.C. Staff in 1943, when the Americans joined us.
- Promoted Group Captain Air Plans in A.E.A.F. (Allied Expeditionary Air Force), and later head of Air Plans to Air Chief Marshal Sir Trafford Leigh-Mallory, November 1943 to 30 September 1944, at Norfolk House, Portsmouth and in France. With Colonel Phillips Melville of the United States Air Force (an Old Harrovian!) was responsible for the production

NOTES ON TOM GLEAVE'S SERVICE RECORD

of the "Overall Overlord Air Plan". T.P.G. wrote it. Phillips Melville criticised. For this T.P.G. was awarded the C.B.E. and the Legion of Merit of the U.S.A. The latter was later changed for the Bronze Star of the U.S.A.
- Became Head of Air Plans, S.H.A.E.F. (Supreme Headquarters Allied Expeditionary Force) under General Eisenhower, 1 October 1944 to 15 July 1945.
- Returned to the Queen Victoria Hospital, East Grinstead, for further plastic surgery, July through to August 1945.
- Appointed Senior Air Staff Officer of the R.A.F. Delegation to France, September 1945 until 3 November 1947.
- Posted to Reserve Command (later Home Command) White Waltham, on 15 December 1947. Filled Staff appointments of Group Captain Organisation, Senior Personnel Staff Officer and Group Captain Auxiliary and Reserves.
- Posted to R.A.F. Staff College, Bracknell, on 7 February 1952 as a member of the Directing Staff. Became a Group Director.
- Invalided out of the Royal Air Force in October 1953, after further plastic surgery at the Q.V.H., East Grinstead.
- Joined the Cabinet Office Historical Section as a member of the Mediterranean and Middle East Team (engaged on the Official Histories of World War II) in October 1953, and completed over 35 years on this task.

Appendix IV

Tom Gleave's Decorations and Awards

C.B.E.
Twice Mentioned in Despatches
1939-45 Star with Battle of Britain Clasp
Aircrew Europe with France and Germany Clasp
Defence Medal
Coronation Medal
Legion of Honour (Officer), France
Croix de Guerre (with Palm), France
Bronze Star of the United States of America
Honorary pilot of the Polish Air Force – awarded 'Wings'
Honorary pilot of L'Armeé de l'Air, France – awarded 'Wings'
Only applicable when visiting Belgium:

    Honorary Citizen of Outre Meuse, Belgium
    Honorary award of the Liége Resistance Medal

Freeman of the City of London
Man of the Year, 14 November 1963
This Is Your Life, first aired in January 1991

Target

Crosby Author's C.B.E.

Honour came to Crosby in the King's birthday list, through the person of Group Captain T. P. Gleave, R.A.F., who has been awarded the C.B.E.

Group Captain Gleave, who is the younger son of Mr. and Mrs. Arthur Gleave, of "Ambergate," Dowhills-road, Blundellsands, is a "regular" R.A.F. officer, having joined on a short commission as far back as 1930. Shot down during the Battle of Britain (on August 31, 1940) he lay seriously ill for many weary months in hospital, and it was during the latter part of this illness, and the ensuing convalescence, that under the pseudonym of "R.A.F. Casualty," he wrote the book, "I Had a Row with a German," which won such approbation from the critics.

Miraculously restored to health, Group Captain Gleave is once again doing full-time work for the Air Ministry, and last year was mentioned in despatches. Now comes this latest honour.

Group Captain Gleave has a wife, and a small son and daughter, who are, at present, living near him in the South.

Group Capt. Gleave

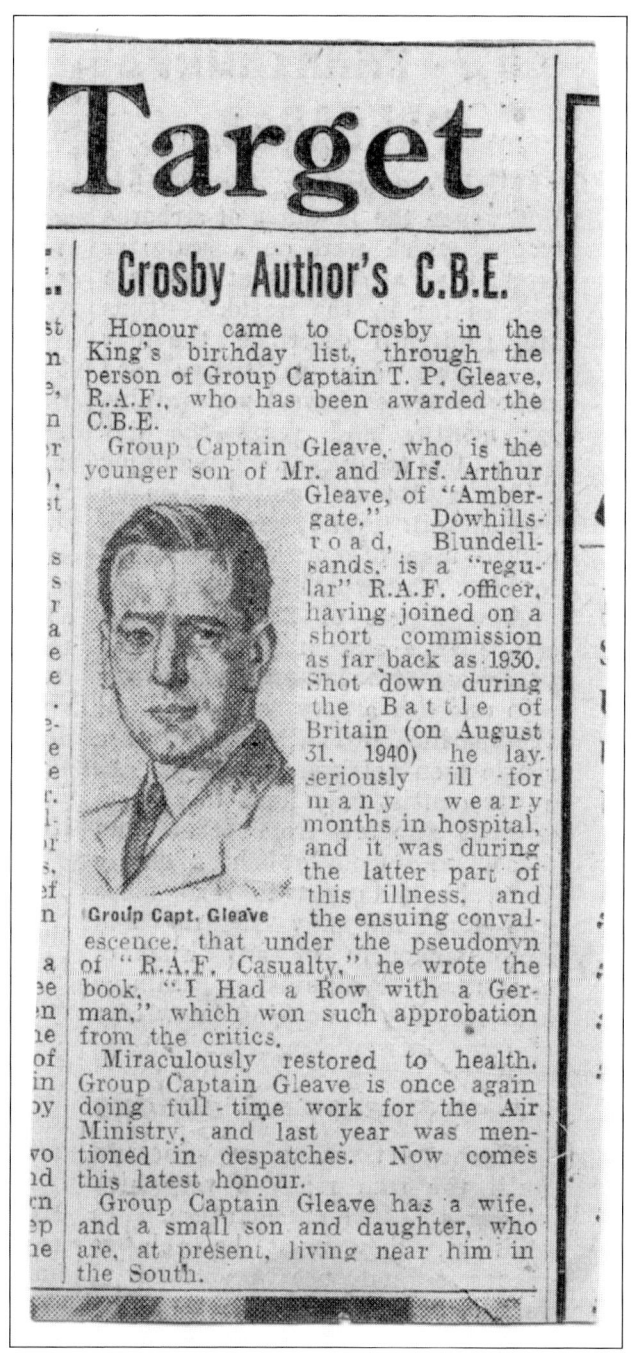

A newspaper cutting that Tom Gleave kept in his records and which contains details of his CBE.